The Art and Science of Writing

A HANDBOOK FOR
HEALTH SCIENCE STUDENTS

Pat Young BA(Hons), MA

Freelance writer and editor, Postgraduate researcher,
Sussex University

CHAPMAN & HALL

London · New York · Tokyo · Melbourne · Madras

Published by
Chapman & Hall, 2–6 Boundary Row, London SE1 8HN, UK

Chapman & Hall, 2–6 Boundary Row, London SE1 8HN, UK

Chapman & Hall GmbH, Pappelallee 3, 69469 Weinheim, Germany

Chapman & Hall USA, 115 Fifth Avenue, New York, NY 10003, USA

Chapman & Hall Japan, ITP-Japan, Kyowa Building, 3F, 2–2–1 Hirakawacho, Chiyoda-ku, Tokyo 102, Japan

Chapman & Hall Australia, 102 Dodds Street, South Melbourne, Victoria 3205, Australia

Chapman & Hall India, R. Seshadri, 32 Second Main Road, CIT East, Madras 600 035, India

Distributed in the USA and Canada by Singular Publishing Group Inc., 4284 41st Street, San Diego, California 92105

First edition 1996

© 1996 Pat Young

Typeset in 10/12 pt Times by J&L Composition Ltd, Filey, North Yorkshire

Printed in Great Britain by Page Bros. Ltd, Norwich

ISBN 0 412 59910 4   1 56593 351 6 (USA)

A catalogue record for this book is available from the British Library

Library of Congress Catalog Card Number: 96–084350

♾ Printed on permanent acid-free text paper, manufactured in accordance with ANSI/NISO Z39.48–1992 and ANSI/NISO Z39.48–1984 (Permanence of Paper).

Contents

Preface

After a long career as an Editor of medical, paramedical, and nursing journals and books, I .was fortunate in being able to realize a lifelong ambition to go to university – to Sussex University, in fact, where I studied English literature as a mature student, both undergraduate and postgraduate. It is on the knowledge gained in both these parts of my life that I have based the contents of this book.

As a student, I found writing essays one of my most difficult tasks, as the approach was so different from my professional writing as a medical journalist. I desperately needed guidance, and in this book I have tried to offer such guidance to health science students in writing scientific prose.

As Editor first of *Physiotherapy* and later of *Nursing Mirror*, I found that both physiotherapists and nurses needed help and encouragement in writing for publication, as literary skills did not always come easily to them. Things have changed over the years, and many more health care professionals now write with skill and confidence, which is as it should be since the exchange of information and ideas is so important in the whole field of medical science.

I hope this book will not only fulfil its purpose of helping health science students to grapple successfully with the written work they must produce during their training, but also inculcate in them a love of our beautiful English language and an appreciation of the elegance of scientific prose. I hope too that, after they have graduated, it will have given them the confidence to continue to practise the art and science of writing throughout their professional careers.

Acknowledgements

I would like to express warm appreciation for his continuing support and encouragement to Professor Norman Vance, of the School of English and American Studies at the University of Sussex, to whom I dedicate this book.

I would also like to acknowledge the help of Rosemary Morris, Associate publisher, Health Sciences, at Chapman & Hall; Professor Michael Whiting, Dean of the Faculty of Health, University of Brighton; Marion Trew, Head of the School of Occupational Therapy and Physiotherapy; Philip Mandy, Deputy Head of the School of Podiatry; and Patrick Saintas, Principal Lecturer in Nursing, all of Brighton University's Faculty of Health.

Finally, my sincere thanks to Dr Robert Mahler, Editor Emeritus of the *Journal of the Royal College of Physicians*, for his guidance and help.

Prologue: an introduction to scientific prose | 1

True ease in writing comes from art, not chance,
As those move easiest who have learned to dance.
Alexander Pope, ' An Essay on Criticism', 1711

One of the briefest and best descriptions of writing is by Stephen Leacock, the humorist who was also Professor of Political Economy at McGill University in Canada. 'Writing is essentially thinking', he remarked in his useful book *How to Write* [1]. He went on to say that all people can think, or think that they can think, but few people can say what they think in language that conveys their meaning to the reader clearly and powerfully.

Students in all branches of the health sciences have obviously got to be able to think clearly, and to communicate their thoughts lucidly in both the written and the spoken word. This is not as easy as it sounds. As the great 18th-century English writer, Alexander Pope, pointed out in his poem 'An Essay on Criticism' (quoted above), it is an art that you have to learn.

Trying to write well is a continual struggle, even for the most experienced, but it is a struggle that is well worth the effort. Bad writing is confused and therefore confusing. Meaning does not emerge clearly from a welter of ill-chosen, ill-ordered words, and the writer merely wastes both his own and his readers' time. One of my favourite pieces of advice to would-be communicators is by Sir Ernest Gowers in *The Complete Plain Words*: 'To be clear is efficient; to be obscure is inefficient'[2].

Scientific prose, in particular, demands of the writer the utmost clarity and accuracy. Science, being the systematic acquisition of knowledge and testing of theories, is a precise discipline. Thus the language in which any scientific principles, methods, or results are expressed must be precise and accurate, leaving no room for doubt or misinterpretation. It follows that a writer of scientific prose must have a good grasp of the basic rules governing English usage, and be able to express the results of a piece of scientific research, for example, in the clearest terms. Efficiency is all-important.

THE ORIGIN OF SCIENTIFIC PROSE

The language that scientists use is spare, economic of words, precise in meaning, and has an austere beauty of its own. But how did this form of prose writing originate? The earliest scientific journals appeared 330 years ago – in 1665. The first two to be published were the *Journal des Scavans*, in France, and the *Philosophical Transactions of the Royal Society of London*, in England.

The articles published in these early journals were couched in straight-forward, descriptive language, but as science progressed so the method of expression for scientific material became more sophisticated. The methodology used in research projects became increasingly important, so a formal pattern for constructing a scientific paper developed following a logical progression, first introducing the particular piece of research and the reasons for conducting it, then describing the methods used and the results obtained, and finally discussing those results and their relative significance. This became known as the IMRAD format, the initials standing for Introduction, Methods, Results, and Discussion.

The IMRAD format made life easier both for authors writing up results of a research project and for editors ploughing their way through a mound of submitted papers. It provided a sturdy framework for the presentation of material, as well as a useful discipline for scientists inexperienced in the art of writing, and it gave editors of scientific journals a basic criterion for accepting or rejecting a paper. An author who accepted the constraints of the framework and used them to the best effect stood more chance of having his or her work accepted than did one whose thinking was illogical and whose presentation was unruly. The IMRAD format has stood the test of time, for it is still used today in scientific journals throughout the world.

SCIENTIFIC PROSE FOR STUDENTS

There is no advantage in waiting until you have graduated, found a job, and begun to think of getting work published, before you study the art of writing scientific prose. The sooner you do the better, both because it will benefit the writing you have to do as a student, and because you will have some experience under your belt when you do come to write for publication. Having work published is, after all, a way of forwarding your career, as potential employers are likely to be more impressed by candidates who have succeeded in convincing a sceptical editor that their work is worth publishing than by those with no published work to their credit. As a student, too, your tutors and examiners are more likely to be impressed by work that is well written and presented than by essays, projects, or examination papers that ramble, are untidy and poorly expressed.

As Stephen Leacock so rightly says, writing is thinking, so the first prerequisite for any kind of writing is to marshal your thoughts, arrange them in a logical sequence, discard those that are irrelevant to your argument, then screw up your courage to put your ideas into words. And it does take courage – and determination, and effort – to start finding the words that will convey your thoughts to the reader clearly and concisely, and then to commit them to paper. The vast majority of professional writers (and I am no exception) find that the most difficult part of writing is to start. Thinking out what you have to say requires a huge mental effort, and the temptation is to prolong that thinking process, or to do yet another bit of research or reading, in order to put off the awful moment when fingers have to meet keyboard, or pen, to transmit those thoughts on to paper. But the reward comes when the words start to flow, however many false starts you may have made, and you realize you have got something to say and the words in which to say it. Then your problem may be knowing when and how to stop!

BACK TO BASICS

Methods of teaching English have varied so much in recent years that it will probably be most helpful to students using this book to go back to the basic rules of grammar, syntax, punctuation, and style, in order to build solid foundations for a good command of the English language. A comprehensive grounding in the basics will benefit any writer, but particularly the writer of scientific prose who must use words sparingly and accurately, and be confident that the meaning they convey is quite clear. In my first editorial job, I worked for a Literary Editor who had a habit late on press day each week of darting out of his cubicle into the main office with one of my pages in his hand and demanding, in agonized tones: 'But Pat, what does this **mean**?'. I had to sit down and rewrite my pearls of prose until he was satisfied that our nine million readers would understand what I meant. I hated him for it, but it was a wonderful training, and a lesson I have never forgotten. So always ask yourself, even if **you** know what you mean, will your readers understand equally well?

There is great satisfaction to be had from honing a piece of writing until you are as sure as you can be that the words you have chosen are the right words to say what you mean, and that you haven't wasted any words in needless elaboration that inevitably obscures your meaning. It is also satisfying to know that you have constructed a piece of prose which is whole – which, as Aristotle commented when he was discussing the art of writing tragedy, has a beginning, a middle, and an end. Prose must have shape and form, like any other art form, and a logical flow that carries the reader along, eager to turn the page until the conclusion is reached. Capturing, retaining, and satisfying the reader's interest is the art of writing, and this is true of both general and specialist writing, including scientific prose.

First things first – the parts of speech | 2

To begin at the beginning: the words we use to form the sentences that express our thoughts fall into different categories, according to the functions they perform. There are eight of them, and they are called the 'parts of speech': nouns, pronouns, verbs, adjectives, adverbs, conjunctions, prepositions, interjections. We will consider them one by one.

NOUNS

A noun is the word used to name a person, object, or abstract idea. There are two kinds of noun: common and proper. **Common** nouns name things that are not special to one person but common to everyone, like a house, or a book, or a coat. **Proper** nouns are particular names for people, or places, or institutions, for example. Your own name is a proper noun because it is particular to you. Proper nouns are spelt with an initial capital letter, while common nouns are not. For instance, you would write: 'I am going to university', using the word 'university' in general terms as a common noun; but 'I am going to the University of Sussex', using the proper noun with an initial capital letter to indicate the title of one particular university.

There are also three different types of common noun: collective, abstract, and verbal.

A **collective** noun describes a group of things or people: i.e. army, jury, crowd, committee, or herd. There are particular collective nouns for particular groups, such as a 'gaggle' of geese; you can have fun inventing your own, and they are all the better if they are alliterative. How about a swot of students, or a pedagogy of professors, for instance?

An **abstract** noun describes a quality or condition – something that is not tangible, such as beauty, wickedness, or emotion.

A **verbal** noun describes an action: i.e. doing, walking, throwing, reading. Adding 'ing' to the main verb turns it into a noun, as well as into the present participle or gerund of the verb – but more of that later.

PRONOUNS

It doesn't take a genius to grasp that a pronoun is a word used for (pro) a noun to avoid unnecessary repetition. Pronouns are divided into seven different categories, according to the job they do:

1. **personal** pronouns, representing the subject (I, we, they);
2. **possessive** pronouns, signifying ownership (my, your, their);
3. **reflexive** and **emphatic** pronouns (myself, yourself, himself), used either as the object of a sentence ('I hate myself'), or to emphasize by repetition ('I did it myself');
4. **demonstrative** pronouns, distinguishing one thing from another (this, those);
5. **interrogative** pronouns, asking a question (which? what?);
6. **relative** pronouns, referring to the noun or pronoun preceding them (who, which, that);
7. **indefinite** pronouns, referring to things vaguely rather than specifically (such, any, some).

Pronouns must always agree with their nouns in matters such as gender, number, and case. For example, gender: the pronoun for a male noun is 'he', for a female noun 'she', and for a neuter thing or object 'it', and they mustn't be confused. Take number: if the noun is singular, then the pronoun must be singular also; and if plural, the pronoun must be plural. Finally, case: if the noun is used in the nominative, accusative, or possessive case, so must the pronoun be also. In the sentence, 'The **men** walked away, then **they** started to run', both the noun and the pronoun are in the nominative case as subjects of the sentence. In 'He saw the **men** and he called **them**' noun and pronoun are in the accusative as objects of the sentence. In 'He found the **men's** luggage and opened **their** suitcases' both are in the possessive, as the luggage belongs to the men.

This is all fairly obvious, but it leads to a difficulty in usage that has been created by the current fashion for sex equality at all costs. The use of the word 'man' or of the male pronoun to signify mankind in general – both men and women – has become unacceptable, and writers often use the plural pronoun 'they' after a singular noun of indeterminate gender, such as 'doctor', in order to avoid using 'he', or the clumsy compromise 'he/she'. There is an easy way round this problem: simply rewrite your sentence using a plural noun in the first place, or use the impersonal pronoun 'one'. It's perfectly possible: just think about it!

VERBS

A verb is a word signifying action of some kind, and is the core of a sentence. In fact, a sentence is not complete unless there is a verb in it. There are two main types of verb: transitive and intransitive.

A **transitive** verb is one that has a direct object: it acts directly upon somebody or something. For example, the verbs 'love' and 'hate' are both transitive, since they both need an object for their action. 'John loves Mary' or 'Jean hates bananas' are both complete sentences, but 'John loves' and 'Jean hates' are statements that are unfinished without objects for the love and hate.

An **intransitive** verb, on the other hand, doesn't require an object because it is complete in itself: 'The bird sings' and 'the sun shines' are two examples. If an intransitive verb is followed by an object, it needs a preposition immediately after it to act as a sort of buffer: for example, 'The sun shines **on** the sea', or 'The bird sings **to** its mate'.

Voice

Verbs have two 'voices', or methods of expression: active and passive. The **active** voice is simple and direct – for example, 'Mary loves Jim' – while the **passive** voice is indirect – e.g. 'Jim is loved by Mary'. In the first example, the subject, Mary, feels active emotion for Jim, the object; in the second, Jim is the subject of the sentence but the passive object of Mary's affection.

You should always use the active voice in preference to the passive if you want to develop a good writing style, because it is simple and direct and easy for readers to understand. Using the passive voice can imply prevarication, or evasion, and can lead to an involved sentence whose meaning is not immediately clear. Never forget that good prose should be easy to read and understand, not difficult and inaccessible; this is particularly true of scientific prose.

Form

Verbs also change their form according to their mood, tense, number, and person.

The **mood** of a verb means the manner in which it is used: to make a simple assertion or ask a straightforward question is the **indicative** mood (I believe you); to give an order or to make an urgent appeal is the **imperative** mood (Believe me!); to express a doubt or desire or to make a condition is the **subjunctive** mood (Would that you believed me).

The **tense** of a verb is governed by time: the period of time – past, present, or future – during which the action it expresses takes place: 'I run' – present tense; 'I ran' – past tense; 'I will run' – future tense.

The **number** of the verb is governed by that of the noun or pronoun that precedes it: a singular noun must be followed by a singular verb, and a plural noun by a plural verb – a simple rule, you would think. You can run into difficulties, however, if you are using a collective noun, such as 'committee', and can't decide whether the verb that follows should be singular or plural. The rule here is to be governed by the sense of what you are saying. If you are referring to the committee as a single entity, perhaps comparing it with other committees, it will be singular; if you are referring to it as a corporate body of individual members, whom you may wish to mention individually, then the noun and the verb should be plural.

The **person** of the verb must also agree with its subject: for example, first person singular ('I am'), or third person plural ('They are'). You would of course never write 'They am', or 'I are' – at least, not unless you were trying to reproduce some very curious vernacular!

The changes in form for changes in number and person are simple and self-evident, but the changes signifying mood or tense are more complex. The indicative and imperative moods are straightforward and self-explanatory (making statements or giving commands), but the subjunctive mood is more subtle. To express doubt or desire, the verb changes its tense to conditional: 'If wishes were horses, beggars would ride' is a good example, as is 'If John were your son, he would be your heir'. There used to be a rule that when the second and third person singular were used, the verb would not agree with the noun but remain in the first person – for instance, 'If he believe' instead of 'If he believes' – though nowadays this rule is rarely observed, being regarded as pedantic. But what about 'God **save** the Queen'?

Finite and infinite

Now we come to finite and infinite verbs. If you look these two words up in the dictionary, you will find that 'finite' means having definite limits (human life is finite, since we all have to die some time), and 'infinite' means having no limits, or extending indefinitely. In grammar, a **finite** verb is one that makes a simple statement which is limited in terms of person and number, and complete in itself, as for instance: 'The sun shines', 'The horse trots', 'The man thinks'. An **infinite** (or non-finite) verb, on the other hand, is one that does not make a complete statement when used on its own, but is open-ended. It needs to be completed by other parts of the verb, such as the infinitive, the participle, the gerund, and the verbal noun, as follows.

'My uncle loves **to sing**' – infinitive.
'My uncle is **singing**' – participle (present).
'My uncle loves **singing** songs' – gerund.
'My uncle loves **singing**' – verbal noun.

Speaking of infinitives, when is it permissible to split one? It used to be a strict rule that an infinitive should not be split in any circumstances: 'to boldly go' would have been considered a heinous infringement of this rule. But in our modern liberal climate it has become almost normal practice to split an infinitive in order to accommodate an expressive adverb between its two parts. Certainly, trying to avoid a split can result in a very clumsy phrase. My own view is that, as always in writing, you should think first of the reader. You should be aiming at writing a sentence with a natural flow that combines correct usage with ease of understanding; if that natural flow is interrupted by placing the adverb in the middle of the infinitive, then don't do it. Likewise, don't split an infinitive if your readers are likely to hold strong and conventional views about this practice: there's no point in antagonizing them. But in general, a simple test of writing style is to read the phrase or sentence aloud to yourself to see how it sounds. Good prose has natural rhythms and cadences, like music, and what sounds pleasing to the ear will also read well on the page.

Weak and strong

Verbs are also divided into two other categories, weak verbs and strong verbs, according to how their past tense and past participle are formed.

The past tense and participle of a **weak** verb are formed by adding the suffix 'ed' or 't'. Examples of this are the verb 'to build' – 'He built' (past tense), 'I have built' (past participle); and 'to love' – 'I loved' (past tense), 'She has loved' (past participle).

The past tense and participle of a **strong** verb are formed by a change of vowel, and sometimes the addition of the suffix 'en' to the past participle. Examples of strong verbs are 'to arise' – 'I arose' (past tense), 'He had arisen' (past participle); and 'to begin' – 'I began' (past tense), 'He had begun' (past participle).

It is sometimes difficult to decide, with a weak verb like 'to learn' for example, whether to add 'ed' or 't' to form the past tense or past participle. The general rule is that you add a 't' for the past tense ('He learnt his lesson'), and 'ed' for the past participle ('I have learned my lesson').

The term 'weak' was originally chosen to describe verbs that needed help to form their past tense and participle, while 'strong' was used for those that needed no such help. They are also called regular (weak) and irregular (strong) verbs.

Auxiliary verbs

The verbs 'to be' and 'to have' are known as auxiliary verbs because they help other verbs along, besides being verbs in their own right. They help to form the present and past tenses of other verbs: for example, 'I **am** going',

'I **have** gone'. Other verbs perform an auxiliary function too: 'shall' and 'will' help to form the future tense, for example.

Not everyone knows how to use 'shall' and 'will' correctly. Here are the rules. When 'shall' is used in the first person ('I shall go', 'We shall speak'), it is forming the future tense of a verb. When it is used in the second and third persons ('You shall go', 'They shall speak'), it forms a promise or threat. 'Will' is used in exactly the reverse way: with the first person it represents a promise or threat ('I will speak'), and with the second and third persons it is part of the future tense ('You/they will go').

Conjugation

I am sure you know how to conjugate a verb. I will simply remind you here that this means to enumerate the forms it takes in its different tenses, or the time-periods which govern it: present, past, and future, and their sub-divisions (e.g. past perfect – 'I had gone'; future perfect – 'He will have gone'). It is as well to be sure of your tenses, so that you always use the right one in the right way.

ADJECTIVES

An adjective is a word that describes or qualifies a noun or pronoun, and adds information or verbal colour to it. Thus you might want to distinguish one kind of light or ink from another by using an adjective to describe its colour – red or green light, blue or black ink. Or you might want to describe a sound with an adjective such as loud or soft, harsh or mellifluous.

While in other languages adjectives are often placed after the noun they qualify, in English they are positioned directly before the noun, when they are called 'attributive': that is, they attribute a particular quality to the noun. They may also be placed after the noun when they are joined to it by a verb, when they are called 'predicative': the predicate is the verbal part of a sentence. Examples are:

'The ugly duckling' – attributive;
'The duckling is ugly' – predicative.

A predicative adjective may be used to qualify a pronoun as well as a noun: i.e. 'It is ugly'.

Comparison

Adjectives are used in their positive, comparative, and superlative forms to describe different degrees of a particular quality. In its **positive** form an adjective simply attributes a certain quality to a noun: e.g. 'The big bang'. In its **comparative** form an adjective implies that a noun possesses more of that quality than does the one it is being compared with: e.g. 'The bigger bang'. The **superlative** form of the adjective is used to denote that the noun possesses more of that quality than any other: 'The biggest bang'.

There are some adjectives which just cannot be compared because there are no degrees of them: 'perfect' is one; 'unique' is another. It is a common error to refer to something as 'quite unique'. This is impossible: a thing is either unique or it is not, as there are no degrees of uniqueness. Similarly perfection is absolute, so you can't say that one thing is more perfect than another. Now try and think of a few more 'absolutes' which do not admit of degrees. What about 'white' and 'black', for instance?

Three main classes

You may not realize that those familiar little words 'the' and 'a' are adjectives. They are called, respectively, the definite and the indefinite article, and they come in the **determinative** class of adjectives: that is, they determine something about the following noun, such as whether it is a specific thing (definite) or just any old thing (indefinite). Other examples of determinative adjectives are 'my', signifying ownership, and 'this', singling out one particular thing.

The second main class of adjective is **qualitative**, associating a particular quality with a noun, as in 'the green door', or 'the beautiful girl'.

The third class is **quantitative**, signifying either a definite quantity (e.g. five, ten, one, none), or an indefinite quantity (much, many, some, few).

Positioning your adjectives

When you use more than one adjective to qualify a noun, be careful that you place your adjectives in the right order. You can give a sentence a very odd meaning if you don't. For example, if you write 'A green lady's sweater', you are implying that the lady is green, not the sweater! But if you write 'A lady's green sweater', no one can mistake your meaning.

Nouns as adjectives

There is no problem about using nouns as adjectives: this is common practice. 'The bus station' or 'the garden centre' are perfectly correct usages. But nouns cannot be used in the comparative or superlative forms of adjective, nor can they be used predicatively, after a verb.

ADVERBS

As an adjective qualifies a noun, so an adverb qualifies a verb, describing its action – e.g. 'He spoke forcefully'. But adverbs can also qualify other words: adjectives ('I am **very** glad'), prepositions ('He is **nearly** on the road'), conjunctions ('It has grown **ever** since I watered it'), and other adverbs ('I accept it **most** gratefully').

Adverbs fall into six different classes according to what they express. This may be:

1. **manner** (how something is done): bravely, generously, gratefully;
2. **place** (direction or position): here, there, somewhere;
3. **time**: yesterday, tomorrow, now, when, always;
4. **quantity, extent, or degree**: twice, nearly, much;
5. **affirmation and negation**: yes, no, certainly, not;
6. **reason and consequence**: why, wherefore, thus, therefore.

Here is a little tip about using adverbs of place when you are enumerating several things in order of precedence – firstly, secondly, thirdly, and so on. It is in fact incorrect to add the ending 'ly', as this is pleonastic, or needless repetition. It is enough simply to write 'first, second, third', and possibly 'last' to show you have reached the end of your list.

Comparison

Like adjectives, adverbs can be used in the positive, comparative, and superlative forms to indicate the degree of an action. Here are examples.

'He ran fast' – positive.
'He ran faster' – comparative.
'He ran fastest' – superlative.

You will note that the word 'fast' can be used both as an adjective, to qualify a noun ('The fast train'), and as an adverb, to qualify a verb ('He ran fast'), and this sort of dual-purpose word adopts the same endings – 'er' and 'est' – to signify the comparative and superlative. An adverb with the ending 'ly' must be preceded by another adverb, 'more', in the comparative form, and by 'most' in the superlative; for example:

'She danced gracefully' – positive;
'She danced more gracefully' – comparative;
'She danced most gracefully' – superlative.

Sometimes an adverb changes completely in its comparative and superlative forms, and these changes are known as irregular forms. The adverb 'well' is typical of this form, as it becomes 'better' in the comparative, and 'best' in the superlative. You will be able to think of several more.

Formation

While many adverbs are formed by adding the ending 'ly' to an adjective, it is worth remembering that certain adjectives may end with 'ly' too: think of 'manly', and 'friendly'. When you want to use such an adjective as an adverb, you can't add another ending to it, so you have to turn it into a phrase, as for instance: 'He behaved in a manly, or friendly, way' (**not** 'manlily' or 'friendlily'!). If you read a lot and come to love the English language, your eye – and your ear – will tell you when to avoid such clumsy formations.

CONJUNCTIONS

A conjunction, as you would imagine, is a word used to join other words or phrases together. The most common conjunctions are 'and' and 'but', but there are several more that will be very familiar to you: 'either', 'or', 'neither', 'nor', 'if', 'that', and 'whether', for example.

Conjunctions are divided into two classes, according to their functions. co-ordinative and subordinative. A **co-ordinative** conjunction joins together words, phrases, or clauses that are independent of each other, while a **subordinative** conjunction joins a dependent clause to a principle clause. Here are examples of the two types of conjunction.

'He opened the window **and** looked out': here 'and' is a co-ordinative conjunction because the two actions of the subject of the sentence are separate, and do not depend on each other.

'He opened the window **as** the room was stuffy': here 'as' is a subordinative conjunction, since the action of opening the window depends on the stuffiness of the room.

You will learn more about clauses and the conjunctions that join them in the next chapter, when we consider how sentences are constructed.

PREPOSITIONS

Prepositions are little words (and they mostly are small) that join nouns or pronouns to other words with which they have some sort of relationship: for example, 'The house **on** the hill', or 'The man **in** the moon'.

There are three classes of preposition: simple, compound, and phrase. **Simple** prepositions are just that – such single-syllable words as 'at', 'by', 'for', 'in', 'of', 'on', 'off', 'to', 'up', 'with'. **Compound** prepositions have more than one syllable, like 'into', 'behind', 'within', 'without', 'inside', 'outside'. **Phrase** prepositions – believe it or not! – consist of more than one word and therefore form a phrase: 'instead of', 'owing to', 'in spite of', 'because of', 'on account of'.

There is also such a thing as a **double** preposition: two prepositions which are used in combination, as in 'from behind the wall', or 'out of the wood'. And last but not least, there is the **participial** preposition, which is the participle of a verb used as a preposition: for example, 'concerning', 'regarding', 'during', 'pending', and 'notwithstanding'.

INTERJECTIONS

To interject means to throw in an abrupt remark, usually while someone else is talking, and an interjection in the grammatical sense is a word of exclamation, such as 'Oh!' or 'Hullo!'. Interjections can consist of more than one word ('Good heavens!'), and swear words or expressions exclaimed in anger or frustration are interjections. However, you would be very unlikely to use an interjection when writing scientific prose; they are much more appropriate to dialogue in a novel or play.

These are the eight parts of speech, and in the next chapter we will look at how they are used to construct a sentence. But first, here are a few exercises to test how much you have absorbed.

EXERCISES

1. Rewrite the following sentence to avoid using a singular noun with a plural pronoun: 'The patient did not want to take their medication'.
2. Should you use a singular or a plural verb after a collective noun?
3. When is it justifiable to split an infinitive?
4. What is the correct use for the auxiliary verb 'shall' and 'will'?
5. What is an 'absolute', and when can it be qualified?
6. Give three examples of irregular verbs, and their comparative and superlative forms.

Building a sentence | 3

Two definitions of a sentence quoted in Fowler's *A Dictionary of Modern English Usage* are admirably succinct [4]. One is: 'A group of words which makes sense'; the other is: 'A combination of words which is complete as expressing a thought'. A sentence combines the various parts of speech to make a statement, ask a question, issue a command, express a wish, or utter an exclamation. Sentences always begin with a capital letter and end with a full stop, a question mark, or an exclamation mark.

There are three kinds of sentence: simple, compound, and complex.

SIMPLE

A simple sentence is just that – a straightforward statement consisting of a subject, a predicate, and usually also an object, with no further embellishment, as for example: 'The man was stroking the dog'. Even if you add adjectives and adverbs to give more colour to it – e.g. 'The kindly man was gently stroking the nervous dog' – the sentence remains simple. An example of a sentence consisting of subject and predicate only is: 'The sun shone brightly', using an intransitive verb (with an adverb) which is complete in itself.

It is surprising how many people write what they think is a sentence and leave the verb out – and I speak from many years' experience as an editor having to correct such bad writing. So it is a good idea to become thoroughly acquainted with the fact that a complete sentence **must** have a subject, a predicate, and usually an object also.

The **subject** is the noun that starts the sentence and initiates or governs the action that follows. The **predicate** is the verb or verbal phrase that expresses the action initiated by the subject. The **object** is what the action is aimed at. Thus, to go back to our man and his dog: the man is the subject of the sentence, initiating the action of stroking that forms the predicate, and the direct object of the man's stroking is – no prizes for guessing – the dog. If the predicate consisted of an intransitive verb, however, any object would be indirect, and joined to that verb by a preposition: e.g. 'The sun shone brightly **on** the man and the dog'. This 'subject, predicate, object' rule doesn't only apply to simple sentences but to compound and complex sentences as well, as we shall see.

One more thing: the subject of a sentence is in the nominative case, and the object is in the accusative case. But the verb 'to be' doesn't take an object, so both the noun that governs the verb and the noun that follows it are in the nominative case. It is important to remember this in case a noun or pronoun changes its form from nominative to accusative. A simple example is: 'It is **I**', which is correctly in the nominative case, while the more commonly used 'It is **me**' is incorrectly in the accusative.

There is, incidentally, such a thing as a 'verbless' sentence. This, to quote Fowler again, is 'a device for enlivening the written word by approximating it to the spoken'[4]. You know the sort of thing: 'No doubt' instead of 'There is no doubt'. You can get away with this if you are using a deliberately conversational style of writing (as I am), but the verbless sentence has little place in scientific prose, which must be resolutely formal.

COMPOUND

Now we have to think about clauses. A clause is a group of words consisting of a subject, predicate, and often direct or indirect object, similar to a sentence but usually forming part of a sentence. Indeed, a simple sentence is sometimes described as the 'main clause', and when two main clauses or simple statements are joined together by a conjunction they become a compound, or double, sentence.

An example is: 'He ran to the door and threw it open'. Another is: 'She was sure of her facts but was too modest to speak'. In both examples each statement can stand on its own, but the second statement is consequent upon the first when joined to it by a conjunction. You will notice that in the second main clause, the subject of the sentence ('he' or 'she') is omitted, to avoid clumsy and needless repetition.

The clauses in a compound sentence are sometimes called 'co-ordinate' clauses, because they harmonize with each other.

COMPLEX

You will all be familiar with the lengthy, tortuous, seemingly interminable sentences which are so verbose that the reader drowns in a welter of words, which are usually so vague in expression that their meaning is almost impossible to divine, and which render the reader word-weary long before the end is in sight. There, that was a fairly complex sentence!

To be complex is, by definition, to be complicated, and such a sentence is composed of a simple main clause complicated by a number of other clauses that depend upon it and interrelate with it and with each other. The trouble is that too many inexperienced writers become punch-drunk with words and write long, complicated sentences with far too many clauses which simply obscure their meaning, believing that this is good writing style. It isn't. This sort of writer would do well to renew his or her acquaintance with the writer's best friend – the full stop.

Subordinate clauses

It is probably most accurate to call all clauses 'subordinate', because they are all dependent on, or subordinate to, the main clause. However, there are three different kinds of subordinate clause, varying according to the job they do.

The **noun clause**, for instance, is a group of words that acts for a noun, frequently as the subject or object of a verb, but sometimes in other ways as well. Here are two examples.

1. 'That he will return your essays is uncertain.' The clause 'that he will return your essays' forms the subject of the sentence, replacing a noun.
2. 'He said that he would return our essays quickly.' Here the clause 'that he would return our essays quickly' is the object of the verb 'he said'.

The **adjectival clause** is a group of words replacing a single adjective in qualifying and describing a noun, as for example: 'The tutor, who was a heavy smoker, had a very nasty cough.' Here the adjectival clause 'who was a heavy smoker' describes and adds to your knowledge about the coughing tutor. This is sometimes called a **relative** clause because it is introduced by a relative pronoun – in this case 'who'.

The **adverbial clause**, as you would expect, takes the place of a single adverb in qualifying, or modifying, a verb. It is usually introduced by a subordinative conjunction, such as 'when' or 'while' or 'until': for example, 'We will wait here until he returns'; or 'I will read while you are writing'.

Now here is a sentence which employs all three types of clause: 'When he read the report, the doctor who was in charge of the patient knew that the prognosis was poor.' The subject of the main clause is 'the doctor', and the verb is 'knew'. The first clause, 'When he read the report', adds to the verb, so is **adverbial**. The second clause, 'who was in charge of the patient', describes the doctor so is **adjectival**. The third clause, 'that the

prognosis was poor', is the object of the verb 'knew', so is a **noun** clause.
That is a complex sentence.

The phrase

A phrase is also a coherent group of words but, unlike a clause, it does not
follow the 'subject–predicate–object' pattern, and it is not complete in
itself. It can be long or short, and can replace any word that is a part of
speech, performing the same function in a more elaborate way. An example
of an adjectival phrase – several words replacing a single adjective – is:
'She sang some remarkably untuneful old songs'. If you add 'rather badly',
you have used an adverbial phrase as well.

Constructing a sentence

A well-constructed sentence must have shape and form, and a certain
rhythm. A short, simple, staccato sentence is effective in grabbing the
reader's attention, but if too many short sentences are used they become
irritatingly repetitious, and recognizably a device. A very long, involved
sentence can be equally boring and irritating, mainly because it is difficult
to understand at first sight and has to be read more than once to absorb the
sense.

I don't need to tell you how to avoid writing too many short sentences,
but it is only too easy, when you are inexperienced, to get bogged down in
a long, tortuous sentence with countless clauses. If you do find you are
rambling on and have lost the thread of your thought or argument, by far
the best thing to do is to use the full stop to break your long sentence up
into two or three shorter sentences. Doing this will also make you concentrate harder on what you are trying to say. If you have written a
sentence that is so lengthy it is almost incoherent, that means that you
have not clarified your thoughts sufficiently well before starting. You have
probably become lazy, self-indulgent, and undisciplined in your thinking,
and your writing is reflecting these failings. Scientific prose must, above
all, be taut and disciplined and clear, so in whatever branch of science you
intend to practise, you must develop taut, disciplined, logical thinking, so
that the sentences you use to express your thoughts will be spare, well
constructed, well argued, and meaningful.

A fine example of an incomprehensible sentence is given in that mar-
vellous little book, *The Complete Plain Words*, by Sir Ernest Gowers: 'The
attitude of each, that he was not required to inform himself of, and his lack
of interest in, the measures taken by the other to carry out the responsibility
assigned to such other under the provision of plans then in effect, demonstrated on the part of each lack of appreciation of the responsibilities vested
in them, and inherent in their positions'[2]. For his translation of this

gobbledygook, Gowers divided the sentence into two, and simplified the wording as follows: 'Neither took any interest in the other's plans, or even found out what they were. This shows that they did not appreciate the responsibilities of their positions.'

It is a good idea to get into the habit of reading your written work to yourself out loud, so that you develop an ear for the natural rhythms and cadences of language. Read passages from feature articles in the 'quality' newspapers to yourself: good journalists, and specialist writers in particular, have to use words concisely and effectively to capture the reader's attention quickly and hold it to the end of their article. It is a very disciplined form of writing, in which every word has to count and any that are redundant must be discarded. Look for articles by named science and health correspondents, and study their writing technique. You will find not a word is wasted in their efforts to get the message, or information, over to readers in a very brief space. Compare this sort of writing with that in any scientific journal, and you will find similarities, although the language used in scientific journals is likely to be loaded with technical terminology, and the articles will be considerably longer.

All science writers have to be precise in their method of expression, whether they are writing for the lay public or for members of their own discipline, and it is this succinct, precise, impersonal style of writing that you, as health science students, have to aim at. The first thing to learn is how to construct a well-formed sentence that is neither too short nor too long, and is easy to understand at first reading. Don't be misled by those academics who believe that prose, to be good, must be inaccessible. I have always maintained that any author who has to obfuscate his meaning with verbiage and jargon either has very little that is meaningful to reveal, or is incapable of expressing himself in direct, simple terms.

Here is a prime example of meaningless verbiage that illustrates my point humorously: 'Gastronomic satiety admonishes me that I have arrived at the ultimate stage of degletition consistent with dietetic integrity.'

In other words, 'I'm full'!

EXERCISES

1. Define a sentence.
2. Which verb does not take the accusative case? Give an example of incorrect usage.
3. Name the different types of clause.
4. What is the difference between a clause and a phrase?
5. What is a compound sentence?

4 | Punctuation – the right stop in the right place

The art of punctuation is one of my minor passions. I call it an art because it requires skill and understanding, and the ability both to know and abide by the rules and to be flexible in their interpretation. It performs the major function of putting the sense into a sentence which without the right punctuation would be nonsense.

I have pointed out the musicality of language – that it has natural rhythms and cadences, like music. To take this analogy further, punctuation marks in writing equate to the rests, or pauses, in music, each one having a different length. The shortest pause is the comma, and the longest the full stop, with the dash, the semi-colon, and the colon in between. Each punctuation mark, or stop, has a specific function and is governed by certain rules, though the rules are not all hard and fast, and personal preference has its place.

Let us consider the various stops one by one: the comma, the semi-colon, the colon, the full stop, the dash, the hyphen, the apostrophe, the quotation mark or inverted comma, the question mark, and the exclamation mark.

THE COMMA

The comma closely follows the full stop as the writer's best friend, since the placing of a comma can alter entirely the sense of a sentence. The comma is possibly the most difficult stop to learn to use accurately and effectively; most writers are either too generous, scattering their commas like confetti, or too mean, hoarding them like gold in a vault. But there are some rules which should help you to know how to use them.

As parentheses

Commas are used in pairs as parentheses, like brackets, to separate a phrase or clause from the rest of the sentence. For example: 'Mr Smith, who suffered from asthma, was wheezing badly.' Here the adjectival clause 'who suffered from asthma' is divided from the main clause by, and contained within, a pair of commas. Both commas **must** be used because they make the meaning of the whole sentence absolutely clear. Leave one or other comma out, and the meaning is obscured.

There are pitfalls in using commas parenthetically, as you will see if you look at the sentence: 'Nurses, whose minds are dull, often make mistakes.' With those two commas in place, the sentence has the offensive meaning that all nurses have dull minds and frequently make mistakes. But take the two commas away and the sense changes to a warning that nurses who allow their minds to become dull are likely to make mistakes. So watch it!

Brackets should be used in preference to commas when the clause or phrase they contain is almost a footnote, an 'aside' that is not strictly part of the sentence but a useful or interesting comment on it.

In enumeration

Commas are used to separate one from another items that are being enumerated in a list, as for example: 'Matthew, Mark, Luke and John'. There is disagreement about the use of a comma before 'and' in such a list: some like it, some don't, and this is where personal preference comes in. Here I have omitted it – against my better judgment, because I am convinced that a comma should always be placed before 'and' for the sake of clarity.

If, for instance, you are listing a number of companies one of which is a partnership, like Marks and Spencer, leaving out the comma before 'and' shows that the two names are linked, while putting it in would separate them. Here is an example: 'Estimates for the building work were received from Brown, Jones, Black and Green'. From this sentence you can't tell whether three or four estimates were received, since Black and Green might (like Marks and Spencer) be partners in one company. If you habitually use the comma before 'and', however, your readers will know that if you leave it out the two names or nouns linked by 'and' are also linked in partnership. That makes sense, don't you think?

After introductions

When you are starting a sentence with an introductory clause or phrase (as I have), you separate that introduction from the clause or clauses that follow with a comma. If you didn't, the sentence would be too long and unwieldy.

If you read it aloud, you will realize that there is a natural pause after the introduction – even if it is only 'Dear Sir' or 'O Lord'.

To break a sentence up

In a compound sentence, a comma is usually placed between the two main clauses that are joined by a conjunction, e.g.: 'The man ran to the wall, and jumped over it'. In a complex sentence containing several clauses, each clause is separated from the others by a comma. Here is an example: 'One of the best books I have read on the subject, which I first read because it was given to me as a prize at school, is written by John Smith, who has a command of language that, in my opinion, is surpassed by none other, although many other books on this topic have been written by more distinguished scholars'. After each clause in that sentence comes a comma, which indicates to the reader that one thought is finished and another is due to begin, though the thoughts are all joined together in one continuous statement. Incidentally, you have probably noticed that I threw in a pair of parenthetical commas as well.

Read that sentence again out loud, and you will get the feel of the brief pauses, or hesitations, that are needed to break the sense up so that it is easier to understand. Then try reading it without any pauses at all, and you will realize how necessary the commas are.

You may well think that the sentence rambles on a bit too much, and you would be quite right. A long-winded sentence with several clauses is often much improved by being ruthlessly chopped into two or more sentences. For instance, here you could change the comma after 'John Smith' into a full stop, and replace 'who' with 'He', so that it would read: 'One of the best books I have read on the subject, which I first read because it was given to me as a prize at school, is written by John Smith. He has a command of language that, in my opinion, is surpassed by none other, although many other books on this topic have been written by more distinguished scholars.' Now you have two self-contained statements that express the meaning more clearly and simply than one long rambling one.

When not to use a comma

As I have already said, commas are too often used too liberally and indiscriminately. My advice is not to use a comma unless you can honestly convince yourself that it is really necessary in order to clarify the meaning of a sentence. Rely on your ear as well as your eye to tell you when a brief pause in your sentence is needed, to separate one thought from another, and slip a comma in there.

A common fault is to interrupt the natural flow of a sentence with a comma for no apparent reason – except, perhaps, that the writer hasn't so far used any punctuation and thinks it is time he or she did. If you look at that sentence again you will see the only punctuation I have used is a dash, to indicate I am going off on another tack, and a pair of parenthetical commas round 'perhaps'. I could have put a comma before 'for no apparent reason', and also one before the final clause 'and thinks it is time he did', but both would have broken up the flow of the sense unnecessarily. The sentence reads better as it is.

In his splendid little book on punctuation, *Mind the Stop* [5], the author G.V. Carey quotes a number of examples from published work of sentences in which commas have been wrongly used, including the following.

'Strangest of all the new sensations, was this uprising of physical virility.' (The comma after 'sensations' interrupts the flow of the sentence unnecessarily.)

'It seems simpler to take one's passport, or, to acquire one.' (The comma before 'or' is fine, but the one after it is redundant.)

'The proposals which, it is believed, Mr Chamberlain is taking with him, are set out in an adjoining column.' (If you use a comma after 'which' there is no need for the comma after 'him'; but if you position the comma **before** which, the comma after 'him' is correct as the second of a parenthetical pair.)

Sometimes a comma is used when one of the other stops is needed. A good example is the following sentence: 'It began to pour with rain, as I had no raincoat I soon got soaked'. The comma here should be replaced with a semi-colon, or a full stop, or with the conjunction 'and'. I would personally prefer the semi-colon, which creates a pause in the sentence instead of breaking it into two, as a full stop would. Using 'and' to join the two parts of the sentence would be perfectly correct, but for my taste is not as elegant as the semi-colon. Here again, you can indulge your personal preference, but elegance of expression is always something to aim for.

THE SEMI-COLON

This is my favourite stop. It is not as functional as the comma, and not as arresting as the colon or full stop. It gives you time to consider what comes next, without acting as a signpost, like the colon, or bringing you to a halt, like the full stop. It is not easy to learn how to use it properly, but it is worth the effort because it brings grace to a sentence.

The semi-colon has two specific uses: (a) to join two main clauses together, providing a longer pause than would a comma and the conjunction 'and'; and (b) to separate two clauses or items that are being enumerated, or listed, after a colon. I will give you examples.

The following sentence from Keith Waterhouse's excellent and very readable book, *English our English*, demonstrates (a) admirably: 'With the merciful decline of over-punctuation, semi-colons are used much less than they were; it is possible, nowadays, to read a magazine from cover to cover without coming across a single semi-colon'[6]. Here he has linked two sentences together, each of which could stand on its own, with a semi-colon because he doesn't want to interrupt the flow of his thought abruptly with a full stop, or to make one very long sentence by using a comma and a conjunction. He has got the balance of the sentence just right by using a semi-colon.

The usage described in (b) is illustrated by the following sentence. 'The workers agreed not to take industrial action on the following conditions: that they would be awarded a 3% salary increase, to take effect immediately; that the increase would be backdated to the beginning of the financial year; that overtime would continue to be paid, at the rates already agreed between the union and management.' This long sentence has to be divided up into a main clause and a number of subordinate clauses, each of them carrying a separate thought but all linked together in one sentence.

Enumeration of items is a common form of presentation in scientific prose. Here is an example adapted from an article published in a medical journal describing a strategy for mental health.

Several areas have been identified for urgent support:

- proper anticipation of risk;
- practical organisational improvements;
- appropriate confidential and professional help for those in distress;
- regular reflection time for learners;
- supervision for clinicians at all stages;
- development of processes of 'internal supervision'.

By setting the very long sentence out in this way, the author (or possibly the journal's copy-editor) has divided it up into easily assimilated clauses which can be used as sub-headings for paragraphs giving additional information. By using first a colon to indicate that information follows, and then semi-colons to mark off each clause, the author has been scrupulously correct in his presentation, but I have to say that not all authors and not all journals follow such a strictly accurate style! You will often see the listed subordinate clauses starting with a capital letter and finishing either with a full stop, although they have no verb and are not complete sentences, or with no punctuation mark at all. This sort of disregard for the rules of grammar and syntax irritates me greatly. Call me a pedant, if you like, but I do think the logic of sentence construction should be observed, particularly in formal scientific prose.

As Waterhouse points out, once you get the hang of the semi-colon it is only too easy to become addicted to it. So beware of the danger of writing long sentences with too many subordinate clauses punctuated with semi-colons, through which the reader has to struggle to reach the end. Be moderate, be considerate, and try not to be self-indulgent.

THE COLON

I have already described the colon as a signpost, and the section on the colon in Fowler's *A Dictionary of Modern English Usage* [4] improves on this idea with the statement that it has 'a special function: that of delivering the goods that have been invoiced in the preceding words'. In other words, it acts as an introduction to an enumeration, or to a quotation, or to an explanation of what has gone before.

We have already seen how it is used to herald an enumeration, in which the individual items or clauses are punctuated by semi-colons. To show how it is used with quotations, I will quote again from Carey's *Mind the Stop*: 'Thus the colon can be appropriately used to separate a clause that introduces a list, quotation, summary, or corollary from the actual list etc itself'[5]. You will see that I have quoted a complete sentence: a colon is always used to introduce a complete statement or passage. But if you look at my first paragraph, you will see that I have introduced the quotation from Fowler without any punctuation. This is because I have quoted only part, not the whole, of the sentence, so that it runs on naturally as part of my own sentence, and does not need to be announced with a fanfare of trumpets, so to speak. A very short quotation which could not be presented as a separate paragraph may be introduced by a comma.

Use of the colon to introduce an explanation of what has gone before is pretty straightforward. Here is an example. 'Academic textbooks are not always easy to read: they are often written in technical jargon; the written text is often interspersed with illustrations, in the form of tables and diagrams, so that its flow is interrupted; and the authors may not have the gift of writing simple, direct prose.' The colon here takes the place of the word 'because', providing a longer pause that indicates to the reader that an explanation making several different points is to follow. The whole, rather lengthy, sentence is broken up by pauses, making it much more readable than if a comma followed by a conjunction had been used throughout.

A colon used sometimes to be followed by a dash (:–) when introducing enumerations, but this combination is tautological – both punctuation marks perform the same function – so has gone out of use.

THE FULL STOP

I describe the full stop as the writer's best friend because it is always used to signify the end of a sentence. The more frequently it is used, therefore, the fewer will be the unnecessarily long-winded sentences written.

The full stop has also, until recently, been commonly used to signify an abbreviation, as in 'The Rev. J. Bloggins', where the full title would be

'The Reverend James (or John or Julian) Bloggins'. In the same way it was used with abbreviated qualifications (M.A. [Master of Arts], or F.R.C.S. [Fellow of the Royal College of Surgeons]), or the abbreviation of titles (B.B.C. – British Broadcasting Corporation). This use of full stops has almost entirely gone out of fashion, and you very rarely see initials or qualifications with full stops nowadays.

Here is a small tip about using initials for abbreviations in a formal piece of scientific prose. One of the most recent abbreviations introduced into health service jargon is 'QUALYs'. Now you may know what those letters stand for, but your reader may not, so before you use them you must write out in full the expression they stand for, and follow that with the initials in brackets, as follows: quality assisted life years (QUALYs). Then, having explained what they stand for, you can go on using the initials only. This is a considerate and useful convention that is well worth remembering.

Three full stops in a row are used to indicate that some words have been omitted from a quotation. Here is a paragraph from an article published in a nursing journal: 'The initial idea for the article arose from talks with student nurses and clinical practitioners engaged in Project 2000 courses'. If you wanted to omit the phrase 'for the article', you would write: 'The initial idea . . . arose from talks'. If you wanted to omit mention of Project 2000 courses, you would write: 'student nurses and clinical practitioners . . .', indicating that the sentence quoted was unfinished. You have to be careful, of course, that the words you omit really are redundant to the sense of your argument.

THE DASH

The dash, like the comma, is often used much too generously, so should be considered with circumspection. It is often used as a parenthesis, like brackets, to enclose a phrase or clause, and it may be difficult to decide whether to use a pair of dashes or a pair of commas – or, indeed, a pair of brackets. As a general rule, the dash should be used either to enclose or to introduce a comment which is in the nature of an 'aside' or an afterthought, as I have used it in the preceding sentence. Like an 'aside' delivered by an actor to the audience in the theatre, it is a comment on the main action but not part of it.

You already know that a pair of parenthetical commas should be used to contain a particular phrase or clause within the main sentence. A pair of brackets should be used in preference to commas when the phrase or clause is subsidiary to the main sentence, containing information or comment that is useful and interesting but not essential to the thought being expressed. Even visually, brackets enclose and isolate the words they contain more explicitly than either commas or dashes.

When the dash is used liberally it conveys a sense of hesitation, as though the writer were continually stopping to gasp for breath before charging off on another tack. It can be used very effectively in fiction or drama when the writer wants to create the impression of a character who lacks the power of concentration, whose mind darts about or, as Stephen Leacock once put it, who 'rides madly off in all directions'. But in scientific prose, whose purpose is to state a thesis and argue it calmly and logically to a thoughtful conclusion, it must be used very judiciously. After all, you don't want your tutors and examiners to think you have a grasshopper mind!

THE HYPHEN

In print, the hyphen looks like the dash in that it is a horizontal line, but it is half the length and has no space on either side of it. This signifies the specific function of the hyphen, which is to join words together when this is necessary to make the sense clear.

There are a lot of composite words which have started out as two separate words, have then been joined by a hyphen, and are now dropping their hyphens and being fused into one single word. Good examples are 'outpatient', 'inpatient', 'suitcase', 'radioactive', 'sittingroom', 'overesti-mate', 'ultraviolet', 'antenatal', and 'postgraduate'. As I have already said, personal preference plays a part in punctuation, and it is the prerogative of the Editor to lay down the 'house style' where choices exist in matters of spelling, punctuation, and general presentation for every journal and book that is published. Opinions differ and fashions change, but in setting the house style for the medical and nursing books and journals of which I was Editor, I always took clarity of meaning as my main criterion, believing that you have no right to waste your readers' time by offering them text which is not clear and cannot be understood at the first reading. Judicious hyphenation is one way of making meaning crystal clear.

Take composite words like those I have quoted above. If you are deciding whether or not to hyphenate, look at the word first with and then without a hyphen, to see which is clearer.

A word like 'co-operate' or 'gastro-intestinal', where two vowels are separated by a hyphen, looks much more comfortable than 'cooperate' or 'gastrointestinal'. And the word 'publichouse' looks pretty odd without a hyphen, doesn't it? The look of a word is an important factor to consider when deciding whether a hyphen is necessary.

The entry on hyphens in Fowler's *A Dictionary of Modern English Usage* [4] states: 'The hyphen is not an ornament but an aid to being understood, and should be employed only when it is needed for that purpose'. One essential use for the hyphen is to join together two, or possibly more, words that are used together adjectivally to qualify a noun – but only when they **precede** that noun. Take the examples 'the well-known scientist' and 'the nineteenth-century poet': placed before the nouns the hyphenated words become composite adjectives, but they change their form if they follow the noun. In 'the scientist is well known', the word 'well' becomes an adverb qualifying the verb 'known', and does not therefore need to be joined to it by a hyphen. Similarly, in 'a poet of the nineteenth century' the word 'nineteenth' stands on its own as an adjective qualifying the noun 'century' and needs no hyphen. This use of the hyphen to create composite adjectives can change meaning completely. Look at the phrases 'the little used car' and 'the hard working man' and you will see what I mean. By inserting a hyphen between 'little' and 'used' you change a small car that is not new into a car that has had little use; and the tough worker becomes a man who works hard. But when a single adjective is preceded by an adverb, as in 'the politically correct practice', it is not necessary to hyphenate because the adverb 'politically' is qualifying the adjective 'correct', not the noun 'practice' that follows, so the two words do not become a composite adjective. Tricky, isn't it?

THE APOSTROPHE

More mistakes seem to be made today with the use of the apostrophe than with any other punctuation mark. How often have you passed a greengrocer with an notice reading 'Ripe tomatoe's' or 'Fresh strawberry's', or read in a newspaper the phrase 'who's name was not given'?

The apostrophe has a very specific function: to show that a letter or letters are missing, and act as a replacement. This most frequently occurs with the verb 'is', when the 'i' is dropped and the 's' is joined to the subject by an apostrophe, as in 'It's' for 'It is', or 'John's coming' for 'John is coming'. An apostrophe is also frequently used before a possessive 's', as an abbreviation of the possessive pronoun 'his', as in 'John's girl-friend', or 'Jean's violin'. The apostrophe is not necessary in complete possessive pronouns such as 'its', 'hers', 'theirs', or 'whose'.

One of the most frequent abuses of the apostrophe is its insertion before a plural 's', as in the greengrocer's 'strawberry's' and 'tomatoe's'. It's quite easy, I suppose, to confuse the possessive with the plural 's', so get it quite clear in your mind that the plural 's' does not, repeat **not**, require an apostrophe, because no letter is missing.

I hardly need to tell you that the word 'not' is often contracted to 'n't', as in 'won't', 'didn't', 'wouldn't', and so on. How many other words can you think of that can be contracted with an apostrophe?

INVERTED COMMAS

Inverted commas are also called quotation marks, as that is what they do – mark a quotation. If you quote a word, a phrase, a piece of dialogue, or a passage from a book, any of which has been written or spoken by someone other than yourself, you must acknowledge the fact by using inverted commas round the words quoted. In a scientific paper, of course, you must also supply the source of that quote to verify it in your list of references – but we will come to the whole question of references and how to present them in a later chapter.

Inverted commas come in pairs, as they must appear before and after the words quoted, and they can also be single or double. They are known in publishing as 'single quotes' or 'double quotes', and it is a matter of house style how you use them. The most common method is to use single quotes first, and if a passage is quoted within a quote, to use double quotes. Here is an example: 'I heard the man say "I'll get you" before he attacked me'. Single quotes are usually used nowadays in preference to double quotes, which are reserved for secondary use. But again, it is for the Editor of a publication to set the house style, and he or she may have a preference for double quotes over single quotes, so before you start writing a formal paper – even a dissertation or a thesis for your degree – it is worth finding out what the house style is for presentation, as good presentation will undoubtedly weigh in your favour.

There is another little problem with inverted commas that you will have to solve: where does the punctuation go – inside or outside the quotation marks? The answer is a logical one. If that passage quoted is part of a sentence, the stop that ends it will come **outside** the quotation mark. If the passage quoted is complete in itself, it will end with a full stop **inside** the second inverted comma. Here are examples.

1. 'In monitoring new drugs, GPs use what is known as "the yellow card system".' In that sentence, the full stop comes after the quotation mark as the phrase 'yellow card system' is part of the overall sentence. (You will also notice that I have used single quotes for the whole sentence, and double quotes for the internal phrase, and that the full stop that ends the sentence lies comfortably between the two.)
2. 'The following sentence is significant. "Cohort studies for the purpose of pharmacovigilance may be either experimental or observational in design."' As a complete sentence is quoted, the final full stop comes inside the double quote, and the final single quote lies up against it. This illustrates the need for both single and double quotation marks, and how they should be used.

Inverted commas are also used ironically, to imply a measure of doubt. The meaning of the words 'The expert said in his evidence . . .' is quite straightforward; but 'The "expert" said in his evidence . . .' immediately expresses doubt about the credentials of the witness. The writer might have said 'the so-called expert' or 'the self-styled expert', but chose the more subtle implication conveyed by the inverted commas. They can be used to identify titles of plays, or pieces of music, or proper names, as for instance 'The Importance of Being Earnest', 'The Ride of the Valkyries', or 'The Connaught Hotel', when such names or titles are not underlined or printed in italics. The choice again is a matter of house style.

THE QUESTION MARK

There is really very little to say about the question mark except that it is placed at the end of a sentence that asks a direct question: e.g. 'Have you finished your essay yet?'. It should not be used with an indirect question, such as 'He asked me what I was doing?'. But I'm sure you know that.

THE EXCLAMATION MARK

There is even less to say about the exclamation mark, which speaks for itself. In journalism, it is popularly known as a 'screamer', which vividly describes its function as an attention seeker. It should only be used in moderation and with circumspection to express surprise, or horror, or amusement, or to give particular emphasis to a statement. You will rarely need to use it in writing scientific prose – unless you have some very remarkable findings to present!

EXERCISES

1. In enumerations, when should you use a comma before 'and'?
2. What are the specific uses for the semi-colon?
3. How is the colon defined in Fowler's *A Dictionary of Modern English Usage*?
4. How should you introduce abbreviations into a scientific paper?
5. What is the correct use of the apostrophe, and when should it not be used?

Developing a good writing style | 5

To have a good writing style means that you write with grace and elegance, with taste and polish, and what you write is clear, simple, well expressed, and easy to comprehend. Indeed, simplicity and clarity are the essence of good writing style.

That great literary figure Sir Arthur Quiller-Couch, who wrote under the pseudonym 'Q' and was Professor of English Literature at Cambridge University for many years, delivered a series of lectures on 'The Art of Writing'[3] to his students which ended with these remarks on 'Style'.

> Essentially it [style] resembles good manners. It comes of endeavouring to understand others, of thinking for them rather than for yourself – of thinking, that is, with the heart as well as the head . . . So your words will be fewer and more effectual; and while you make less ado, what you do will be more profitable.

Quiller-Couch chose four epithets to describe good style: appropriateness, perspicuity, accuracy, and persuasiveness. They can all be applied to scientific prose.

Appropriateness

The style of writing must, of course, be appropriate to the particular subject matter the writer is concerned with, and the style most appropriate to any science subject is scientific prose.

Perspicuity

As Quiller-Couch put it: 'The more clearly you write the more easily and surely you will be understood'. By writing simple, direct prose, using the active voice, choosing short, familiar words, and constructing uncomplicated sentences, you are developing a perspicuous writing style which is very appropriate to scientific prose.

Accuracy

There is no place in science writing for vagueness, slovenliness, or laziness. Accuracy is paramount, but it demands care, effort, and concentration. You insult your readers if you cannot take the trouble to be accurate – and you undermine the credibility of your thesis.

Persuasiveness

Persuasion, according to 'Q', cannot be achieved without a sense of beauty. By this he meant the grace and elegance of expression that can add charm to an otherwise unattractive piece of prose; the rhythm and musicality that make prose writing euphonious – even poetic. An elegantly expressed sentence will present an argument far more persuasively than one which is badly written and difficult to understand.

GENERAL RULES FOR GOOD STYLE

There are five recognized principles to follow for good style.

1. Prefer the familiar word to the far-fetched.
2. Prefer the concrete word to the abstract.
3. Prefer the single word to the circumlocution.
4. Prefer the short word to the long.
5. Prefer the Saxon word to the Romance.

The familiar word

Don't be misled into thinking that scientific prose must be full of technical terminology and jargon. Too much of it is, and editorial staff working on scientific books and journals have to spend far too much time trying to unravel and interpret material written in obscure language. Obscurity of expression is not a sign of an impressive intellect but of an inability to think clearly and communicate ideas simply. So don't be tempted to use an unfamiliar word or expression in place of one that is readily recognized: to write, for example, 'olfactory acuity' instead of 'sense of smell'.

The concrete word

If you consult your dictionary for definitions of 'concrete' and 'abstract', you will find that 'concrete' means real, actual, and tangible, while 'abstract' refers to a quality or state, an idea rather than a thing, something intangible or immaterial. Thus a concrete word will have a precise meaning, while the meaning of an abstract word will be inevitably somewhat vague. In writing scientific prose you must strive at all times to be precise in your meaning, so this rule has a specific application for you. This is not to say that you will never need to use words that have an abstract meaning, or discuss abstract ideas. The familiar expressions 'quality of life' and 'level of consciousness', which are in everyday use in the field of health care, are both intangible and abstract.

The single word

A besetting sin of writers – of which I am as guilty as anyone – is to use more words than are necessary to convey meaning. You will be familiar with those bureaucratic phrases such as 'in respect of', 'in relation to', 'with regard to', and 'in terms of' which can – and should – be replaced by a single preposition. The phrases I have quoted are circumlocutions in that they go round the point instead of straight to it. Look at the sentence (taken from Gowers' *The Complete Plain Words*): 'There may be difficulties with regard to the provision of suitable staff'. How much more to the point is: 'It may be difficult to provide suitable staff'[2].

The short word

Short words, as with short sentences, are always preferable to long ones, but in scientific writing it may be necessary to use long technical words because of their precise meaning. In general, however, it is better to use a short word that is familiar and therefore easily understood than a longer, more abstruse one with which the reader may be unfamiliar.

The Saxon word

This is a rule which you may happily ignore, since so much medical and scientific terminology has its roots in Latin, which was the begetter of the Romance languages, such as French, Spanish, and Italian. The Fowler brothers (H.W. and F.G.), who laid down these five principles in their classic book *The King's English*, remark that this one is the least important, since 'the writer whose percentage of Saxon words is high will generally be found to have fewer words that are out of the way, long, or abstract, and fewer periphrases, than another'[8]. In other words, if a writer abides by the first four principles, he or she is likely to use more words derived from the Saxon language than from Latin.

CHOOSING THE RIGHT WORDS

When you have marshalled your thoughts and organized your material, and are starting on your essay, project, research paper, or whatever it may be, the first thing you have to be sure of is that you are choosing the right words with which to express your ideas. This may sound blindingly obvious, but it is surprising how many words are continually confused with other words which are similar but have a different meaning. Think of 'alternately' and 'alternatively', 'practical' and 'practicable', 'militate' and 'mitigate', 'disinterested' and 'uninterested'. Are you quite sure what each one means?

'Alternately' means by turns, while 'alternatively' means as another option. 'Practical' means to be useful in practice, while 'practicable' means possible to do. To 'militate' against something means to put an obstacle in the way, while to 'mitigate' means to lessen the effect. 'Disinterested' means to be objective, to have no personal bias, while 'uninterested' means indifferent or unenthusiastic. If you are not absolutely sure of the meaning of a word, look it up in the dictionary straight away. There is no shame in having a well-thumbed dictionary; indeed, it is the sign of a humble and conscientious writer.

ARRANGING THE WORDS PROPERLY

This piece of advice may also seem insultingly obvious, but you may be surprised to know how the meaning of a short, simple sentence can be changed when the words are placed in a different order. Altering the position of a single word can make all the difference. Take the word 'only', and the statement 'I saw his brother last week'. 'I saw his only brother last week' means that the person of whom you are speaking has just one brother and no more. 'I saw only his brother last week' implies you saw no one else – though there could be other brothers whom you didn't see; while 'I saw his brother only last week' tells your reader how recently you saw his brother. By placing 'only' in three different positions, you give that little sentence three different meanings.

There is a hackneyed but amusing example of badly arranged words which gets the point over well: 'If the baby does not thrive on raw milk, boil it'; not to mention the official request to 'return notification of the birth of twins in the attached envelope'. And what about 'Would you rather a lion ate you or a tiger?'; or 'For sale, a piano, property of a musician, with carved legs'? All these comic sentences can be easily corrected by rearranging the words. The rule to follow is that the words that are closely related to each other should be placed as near to each other as possible.

Sometimes it may be necessary to reorganize completely a lengthy complex sentence whose plethora of subordinate clauses has separated subject from verb and verb from object so that the thread of sense is broken. You know the sort of thing I mean: 'Nurses who have taken a specialized training course which does not lead to a recognized additional qualification but which does offer to successful course members a certificate of competence in that specialty will, in certain circumstances and provided there are suitable vacancies on the staff of a specialized unit, be able to find employment in such a unit'.

The way to reorganize such an unwieldy sentence is first to decide what is its main point, then to put that point at the beginning, and follow it with the explanation. Here we go: 'Nurses may be able to find employment in specialist units if they have a certificate of competence in that specialty and if suitable vacancies exist'. That's better, isn't it? It's all a matter of getting your thoughts in a clear order and then expressing them precisely and logically.

JARGON

What exactly is jargon, and why should a good writer avoid it at all costs? My dictionary gives a very good answer with its definition: 'confused, unintelligible, outlandish or barbarous language'. And that, as Lady Bracknell might have said, is all that can be said about jargon!

But it's not quite all, of course. Every profession or occupation has evolved its own technical jargon or terminology which acts as an internal language for practitioners of that profession. If you are writing for professional colleagues you must, naturally, use the technical terminology which carries a precise meaning for them, rather than translate it into lay language whose meaning may be less precise, and which may imply that your readers are not capable of understanding the correct technical terms. On the other hand, there is no point in indulging in verbose technical terminology just to impress your readers with your knowledge, if a simpler method of expression will suffice. I quote you a good example of unnecessary technical verbiage from the medical journal *The Lancet*.

Experiments are described which demonstrate that in normal individuals the lowest concentration in which sucrose can be detected by means of gustation differs from the lowest concentration in which sucrose (in the amount employed) has to be ingested in order to produce a demonstrable decrease in olfactory acuity and a noteworthy conversion of sensations interpreted as a desire for food into sensations interpreted as a satiety associated with ingestion of food.

The translation for this periphrastic passage, originally quoted in Gowers' *Complete Plain Words* [2], was also supplied by *The Lancet* to show the style it preferred:

> Experiments are described which demonstrate that a normal person can taste sugar in water in quantities not strong enough to interfere with his sense of smell or take away his appetite.

That is a really elegant piece of scientific writing: formal without being portentous, conveying information in simple, jargon-free language that makes the meaning clear. Use it as a model for developing your own style of writing, and you won't go far wrong.

EXERCISES

1. How did Sir Arthur Quiller-Couch define style?
2. Which four epithets did he use to describe good style?
3. Which of the five rules for good style can you disregard, and why?
4. Give two pairs of words that are frequently confused?
5. Define the term 'jargon'.

Some sins and solecisms | 6

SOLECISMS

It is comforting to know, when you are struggling to get your thoughts down lucidly and accurately on paper, that there are certain mistakes, or solecisms, that an awful lot of writers make; by knowing what they are you can learn to avoid them yourself. We have already looked at some of them, but there are several more which are well worth thinking about. So let's have a short refresher course on commonly made mistakes.

Ellipsis

This term is used to describe the common error of leaving out a word or two that are essential to correct construction. An example is: 'I think I write as well, if not better, than he does'. The second 'as' in the phrase 'as well as' has been omitted; the sentence should read: 'I think I write as well **as**, if not better than, he does'. Both positive and comparative phrases (as well as, better than) must be complete to make the construction correct.

Tautology

This means saying the same thing, using a word needlessly that has the same meaning as the word that precedes or follows it. My favourite example is 'the true facts'. If a fact is not true, it is not a fact, so the word 'true' is redundant and therefore tautological. And what about 'refer back'?

Pleonasm

This is very similar to tautology, but the subtle difference is that it means using more words than are needed to convey the sense intended. Thus the sentence, 'The vote was carried unanimously by everyone present', is a pleonasm because the phrase 'by everyone present' means the same as 'unanimously', so is redundant.

Unrelated or unattached participle

This fault is sometimes also called the 'hanging' or 'dangling' participle, and it occurs when a participle (part of the verb) is not attached to the noun or pronoun which should be the subject of that verb. Here is an example. 'Having made enquiries at the university bookshop and library, there is no similar book written specifically for students.' Who made enquiries at the bookshop and library? The participial phrase 'having made enquiries' is left hanging without a related noun or pronoun to follow it. The sentence should read: 'Having made enquiries at the university bookshop and library, **I found that** there is no similar book written specifically for students'.

Double negative

You would never make the mistake of writing 'I don't know nothing about this subject' – but you might be misled into writing: 'I wouldn't be surprised if he doesn't return my essay'. There is a double negative in both sentences. None of the negatives is necessary because positive statements, such as 'I know nothing about this subject', are much more telling.

Split infinitive

We have already decided that to split or not to split an infinitive is now a matter of personal choice, though once there was a strict rule that an infinitive should never be split. But I hope you agree with me that to split an infinitive for no good reason verges on verbal vandalism! The sense and sound must always come first. An infinitive can be greatly enhanced by an adverb which follows it immediately, giving it added colour and life; if that same adverb is interposed between the two parts of the infinitive, the sense is interrupted, the colour is lost, and the sound is uneasy. To misquote Dylan Thomas's poem slightly, 'To go gently into that good night' has far more colour and rhythmic flow than 'To gently go into that good night'. Do I make my point?

Qualifying the absolute

I would remind you that there are certain words whose meaning is absolute, and cannot be qualified by degrees. There are no degrees of white or black, for example; anything in between is a shade of grey. So beware of saying something is 'quite unique': either it is unique, meaning a one-off with no like or equal, or it is not.

Ending a sentence with a preposition

This is a rule which it is sometimes difficult not to break, but no sentence should end with a preposition. This is because the final word in a sentence is important and carries emphasis, and a preposition is a small, unpretentious word not capable of bearing such responsibility. 'This is the cupboard which I left my coat in' is a weaker statement than 'This is the cupboard in which I left my coat'. But that great master of the written and the spoken word, Sir Winston Churchill, made gentle fun of this rule when he wrote: 'This is the sort of English up with which I will not put'.

The case of the pronoun

When a pronoun is the object of a sentence, rather than the subject, it changes its form from the nominative case (he, who) to the accusative case (him, whom). Thus it is correct to say 'He (nominative) saw him (accusative)'. But the verb 'to be' is an exception: both its subject and object take the nominative case. It is incorrect to say (as most of us would), 'It's him', or 'It's me'; to be pedantically accurate, you should say 'It's he' or 'It's I'. You can get away with the inaccurate accusative in colloquial speech, but if you are writing formal prose you must be careful to get your cases right. For example, in the sentence 'The patient who the doctor examined this morning has been discharged', the relative pronoun 'who' is wrongly in the nominative; it should, of course, be 'whom' as the object of the doctor's examination. And don't forget that the preposition 'to' takes the accusative: e.g. 'To **whom** did I give the case notes?'

Concord

The rule of concord means that perfect harmony must prevail within a sentence: words that are related to each other must agree with each other in gender, number, and case. Too often, however, discord reigns as the writer forgets that a singular noun must be followed by a singular verb and a singular relative or possessive pronoun. One of the most common mistakes is to follow a singular noun with a plural pronoun, as follows: 'The patient did not want to take their medication'. This, as we saw in an earlier chapter, is often done to avoid using the clumsy 'his/her' when the gender of the subject is uncertain, but it breaks the rule of concord. There are ways of getting round the problem, perhaps by omitting the possessive pronoun: 'The patient did not want to take any medication'. Verbs should also always agree in number with their subjects, but one has to decide whether to use a singular or a plural verb after a collective noun, such as 'the crowd'. The rule is to use the singular when you are thinking of the collective noun as a whole entity ('the crowd has demonstrated angrily'), but the plural if you are thinking of its individual members ('the crowd were scattered in all directions').

Using the right preposition

There are certain words which should traditionally be followed by certain prepositions: examples are 'different **from**' and 'averse **to**'. But the use of 'different to' and 'different than', and 'averse from', is creeping insidiously into our language, until it is difficult to know which usage to adopt. So how do you decide which preposition to use if you are not sure which is correct? My advice is first to look the word up in your dictionary, where you should find guidance on the preposition that should follow it. If you are still not sure, try a reference book on English usage, such as Fowler's *The King's English*, Eric Partridge's *Usage and Abusage*, or *The Oxford Dictionary for Writers and Editors* (see 'Further reading'). Beware, too, of the current habit of using the wrong preposition to follow a verb. When I hear people saying 'I am fed up **of**' instead of 'I am fed up **with**', or 'I convinced him **to**' instead of 'I convinced him of the need to' or 'I persuaded him to', I get very irritated.

Sequence of tenses

Many people forget the rule that a certain tense used in the main clause of a sentence must be followed by a certain tense in a subordinate clause; this is known as the sequence of tenses. The rule is confusing because it only applies to one tense: the past tense in the main clause must be followed by the past tense in the subordinate clause. Thus you would write: 'I discovered that he knew where the library was.' The present or future tenses when used in the main clause may, however, be followed by any tense in the subordinate clause.

Who, that, which

Not everyone is sure what is the right relative pronoun to use to introduce a subordinate clause, and in particular when to use 'which' and when 'that'. The answer lies in the antecedent. If the antecedent is a person, the correct pronoun is 'who'; if it is a thing, either 'that' or 'which' may be used, with the proviso that 'which' should refer specifically to an inanimate object, while 'that' should refer to an organization, institution, or anything with human connotations. It is thus correct to write 'The man who . . .', 'The university that . . .', and 'The book which . . .'. If, however, there is no antecedent, it is correct to use 'and this' rather than 'which': for example, instead of 'His foot slipped, which made him fall' you should write: 'His foot slipped, **and this** made him fall'.

Distributive pronouns

Those little words 'each', 'either', and 'any' are termed 'distributive' pronouns, and are governed by certain rules. For example, 'either' can only refer to one of two alternatives (either one of the two sisters), while 'each' and 'any' can refer to an unlimited number of alternatives (each of the five brothers, any of the twenty students). All three distributive pronouns must be followed by a singular verb and possibly pronoun, as they are all themselves singular: 'Each of the students thinks that he is right'.

Words commonly misused

In the chapter on style, we have already looked at the importance of choosing the right word, and at pairs of words that are commonly confused with each other because they are similar. Here are some more pairs of words that are often wrongly used because their meaning is similar.

'Lay' and 'lie': hens lay eggs, people lie in their beds. 'Lay' is also the past tense of 'lie', and 'laid' the past tense of 'lay': 'They lay on the ground for days'; 'The hens laid well last week'.

'Less' and 'fewer': less refers to quantity, and fewer to number. Thus 'There was less blossom on the trees this spring, so there will be fewer plums to pick in the autumn'.

'Like' and 'as': like (as well as being a verb) is an adjective, while as is a conjunction, so they have different functions. You should not write: 'He did like he was told'; you should write: 'He did **as** he was told'.

'Due to' and 'owing to': due to should be used after a noun, and owing to after a verb. For example: 'The accident was due to careless driving'; 'He fell owing to his loss of balance'.

'Compare to' and 'compare with': you compare two different things **to** each other when you are suggesting there may be a likeness between them; you compare two similar things **with** each other to discover their differences.

Nouns as verbs

The increasing practice of creating new verbs by adding the suffix 'ize' to nouns is a particularly unwelcome one. It should be resisted at all costs, even though it does save words. The verb 'prioritize' – meaning to set one's priorities – has crept into everyday usage. An even uglier one I heard recently is 'concretize', presumably meaning to turn abstract ideas into concrete plans. Don't do it! In this instance, be generous with your words instead, so as to make your meaning clearer and not to mangle our beautiful English language.

Nouns as adjectives

The practice of using nouns as adjectives has prevailed in scientific writing for a good many years, and is less unwelcome than using nouns as verbs, though it is still to be discouraged. It is a sort of verbal shorthand: for instance, it is quicker to write 'The Natural History Museum' than 'The Museum of Natural History' – though the latter is, strictly speaking, more correct and certainly more euphonious. I am reminded of the eminent surgeon asking the medical student (in Richard Gordon's novel *Doctor in the House*): 'What's the bleeding time?'. It's not surprising he was told the time of day rather than the time the blood took to coagulate.

SOME SINFUL HABITS

Having looked at solecisms, or errors in grammar and syntax, now let us look at some sins or bad habits that writers often fall into. If you want to write good scientific prose, try not to commit these sins; if you have already developed these bad habits, try to purge yourself of them.

Poor spelling

A piece of text that contains spelling mistakes is an insult to the reader. It means that the writer is either lazy, and hasn't bothered to check his or her spelling with the dictionary, or arrogant, and doesn't think he or she needs to. A lot of people find it difficult to spell correctly, I know, but the trick is to develop a visual memory, to read a lot, and to memorize how words are spelt. I am lucky in having few problems with spelling, and I am sure it is because I have a visual memory for words and can see them in my mind's eye before I write them down. If you are writing with a word processor, of course, you can get it to check your spelling for you, but it is really better to try and get it right yourself, rather than to depend on a computer to do the work for you. It's good mental discipline, which is important in science, as well as good practice in memory training.

As well as learning to visualize words in your mind, you can work out little tricks for spelling those words that always give you trouble. Words that are similar but have different meanings, such as 'principal' and 'principle' or 'stationary' and 'stationery', are notoriously difficult. If you remember that 'principal' is an adjective, you can take the 'a' as a link which will remind you to spell it with an 'a'. In the same way, if you think of a stationer's shop where you would buy paper, envelopes, and other stationery, you will know it should be spelt with an 'e'. It can be fun working out your own tricks for correct spelling, and once you have got them into your head they will stay there and make life much easier. But if you have any doubts at all, **consult the dictionary**!

Clichés

This seems to be the age of the cliché. One has only to turn on the radio any day to hear them pouring out of the mouths of broadcasters of all persuasions – though politicians are the worst offenders. 'Having said that', 'at this moment in time', 'a level playing field', 'the hidden agenda', 'the bottom line', 'if you like', 'window of opportunity', 'no way', 'whatever', are all hackneyed phrases which come under the heading of 'cliché'. I'm sure you can think of many more that are just as irritatingly meaningless.

A cliché is a word or phrase that is overworked because it has become too popular. It may once have had some value, but that value has been lost through constant repetition, often out of its proper context. To avoid using clichés, the writer must try to be original in his or her use of language, and not be tempted to use expressions or phrases that have been prefabricated by other writers. Scientific prose is not exempt from cliché: think how the word 'process' is being overworked in phrases such as 'the disease process', 'the nursing process', 'the healing process'. Soon it will lose its meaning altogether.

Colloquialisms and slang

Scientific prose is essentially formal and impersonal, so colloquialisms and slang, which both belong to a conversational style of writing, are out of place. The only exception would be in presenting a case history, where you might want to quote what a patient had said, when you would naturally repeat the colloquial language the patient had used to make a particular point about his or her behaviour or method of expression. Similarly, in general prose it is best only to use slang and colloquialisms for a specific purpose, and with circumspection.

Jargon and gobbledygook

We know that every profession and occupation has its own jargon, which should be used only to communicate with colleagues with the same training, experience, and knowledge of the technical terminology. Even then the technical terminology should be simplified where possible, and only used when it conveys a precise meaning that cannot be conveyed in simpler language. Gobbledygook – a vividly descriptive term derived from the sound that turkeys make – is different from jargon in that it employs a plethora of ordinary words rather than technical terms to confuse the reader. It is verbosity used to obscure meaning and to conceal a lack of knowledge and clear thinking. You would never be guilty of this sin, I am sure.

EXERCISES

1. What is the difference between tautology and pleonasm?
2. What is a 'hanging participle'?
3. Why should a sentence not end with a preposition?
4. What is the rule of concord?
5. When should you use the pronouns 'who', 'that', 'which'?

Figures and flourishes |

Before we move on to consider the conventions of scientific prose and the construction of a scientific paper, let us spend a little time looking at some of the methods of expression you can use to heighten your meaning or make it more vivid. Some of them come under the heading 'Figures of Speech'; others I have called 'Flourishes', as they are ways of ornamenting or embellishing your prose. You are probably familiar with some of the figures of speech, for instance simile and metaphor, but those with obscure names derived from Greek, like litotes, oxymoron, and onomatopoeia, may not be so familiar. They are perhaps more applicable to the literary art than to the craft of scientific writing, but they make interesting acquaintances, and you never know when you might find them useful.

FIGURES OF SPEECH

The so-called figures of speech can be roughly divided into four groups: those that are based on similarity, those based on contrast, those based on association of ideas, and those that come under the convenient heading of 'various'. We will start with similarity.

Simile

When you write 'She shook like a jelly', or 'He played like an angel', you are using similes to compare one thing with another in order to create a vivid verbal impression. The less alike the two things compared are, the greater will be the effect. Similes are usually introduced by the words 'like' (as above), and 'as', as in 'He turned as green as a gooseberry'. Try and make your similes really original and unusual, and beware of the similes that have become clichés: 'drunk as a lord', 'cold as charity', 'like water off a duck's back' are examples. The two I have used to start with aren't exactly original either!

Metaphor

The difference between metaphor and simile is that while simile makes a specific comparison between two things, metaphor only implies a resemblance. It draws an analogy between two things by substituting a description of one for another. An example of metaphor is 'the ship of State', which implies that a State or nation is like a ship which requires a captain and crew (a government) to sail it. Other familiar metaphors are 'water under the bridge', implying that something has passed and will not return, and 'playing the trump card', meaning that the action wins over any competition. Beware of using what is called a 'dead metaphor' – one that is no longer valid; and of mixing your metaphors. The best example of mixed metaphor I have seen is the classic: 'I smell a rat; I see it floating in the air; I will nip it in the bud'. The writer of that sentence managed to mix three metaphors together.

Allegory

An allegory is really a sustained metaphor: a story told about a fictitious character in a fictitious situation in order to draw a telling parallel with a real-life situation. One of the greatest allegories in our literature is John Bunyan's *Pilgrim's Progress*. In the same category come parable and fable, a parable being a story about familiar people and objects intended to convey a spiritual or moral truth, and a fable a story endowing animals and inanimate objects with the ability to speak and act like humans.

Personification

As in fables, this is the literary practice of making 'dumb' creatures and inanimate objects behave like human beings. The best example of a modern fable using personification I can think of is George Orwell's *Animal Farm*, in which the animals assume human qualities so that they can force the human farmer to leave, and learn how to run the farm themselves.

Antithesis

Now we move on to contrast, and the use of two phrases or expressions in direct opposition to each other to give more power to meaning. A thesis is the first statement, or proposition, of an argument to be proved by reasoning; an antithesis is the second stage of the argument putting the opposite point of view. The figure of speech known as 'antithesis' opposes two thoughts in one sentence: for example, 'Man proposes, God disposes'.

Oscar Wilde was a master of antithesis; think of the lines from *Lady Windermere's Fan*, 'I can resist everything except temptation'.

Irony

Perhaps the most famous example of irony comes in Mark Antony's great speech, beginning 'Friends, Romans, countrymen', in Shakespeare's play *Julius Caesar*: 'For Brutus is an honourable man; so are they all honourable men'. Mark Antony was delivering a funeral oration over Julius Caesar's body, whom Brutus and his fellow murderers had assassinated; his apparent praise was not intended to be taken literally, but as a heavily ironical attack upon Brutus. So irony, put simply, is saying one thing but meaning the exact opposite.

Litotes

This is an ironical understatement using the negative to convey the opposite meaning, as in 'It's not bad', meaning it's good, or 'She's not a bad looker', meaning she's extremely good-looking. But beware of using this sort of double negative – 'It's not unusual', or 'It's not unlike' – too lavishly, because qualifying statements continually in this way can imply the lack of courage to make a direct statement.

Metonomy

This figure of speech uses a word or words closely associated with a particular thing to describe that thing. A typical example is using the word 'crown' – an attribute or symbol of the monarchy – in place of the word 'monarchy'. The familiar aphorism, 'The pen is mightier than the sword', is a good example of metonomy.

Synecdoche

This figure is also based on association of words, but uses a word describing part of something to represent the whole: for example, 'sail' instead of 'ships', or 'hands' instead of 'crew'. If you refer to your favourite football club by its location only – i.e. Chelsea or Leeds – you are using synecdoche.

Climax

Moving on to the 'various' figures of speech by which meaning can be enhanced, there is the device of building a sentence to a climax by making statements of increasing intensity or strength. Julius Caesar's triumphant remark, 'I came, I saw, I conquered' (*Veni, vidi, vici*), is a classic example of climax.

Hyperbole

This is the deliberate use of exaggeration to increase emphasis. I suspect the word 'hyperbole' provides the derivation of the current slang term 'hype', though my dictionary says its origin is unknown. However, since any unrealistically extravagant statement, such as 'I nearly died laughing' or 'I've been there thousands of times', is using hyperbole, it's not impossible that 'hype' – which means extravagant publicity – amounts to much the same thing.

Euphemism

When you want to disguise something disagreeable, you may use a word for it that has a more pleasing ring to it: this is a euphemism. There are plenty of euphemisms for the place where we relieve ourselves: toilet, lavatory, powder room, ladies, gents, convenience, loo – I'm sure you can think of plenty more. Other euphemisms that spring to mind are 'passing over' for dying, and 'vertically challenged' for restricted growth. Euphemism is not to be confused with 'euphuism', which means an ornate or artificial style of writing or speaking.

Oxymoron

An effective way of grabbing the reader's attention is by using two words together which have opposite meanings: this is oxymoron. The 'gentle giant' and the 'wise fool' are typical examples, though an imaginative writer will think of sharper contrasts and more absurd contradictions to create an effect.

Onomatopoeia

There are many words which imitate the sound of something, like thud, hiss, boom, croak, whisper, and sizzle. Using a word to resemble a sound is onomatopoeia.

Alliteration

Using several words in succession with the same initial consonant or vowel is a literary device known as alliteration. It is employed to the best effect in verse.

FLOURISHES

Elegant variation

It is dull and boring to read a sentence or paragraph in which the writer has used the same word over and over again when it would have been possible, with a little effort, to find other words with a similar meaning to replace it, and make the passage more varied and readable. This is known as 'elegant variation': the practice of using substitutes for a word to avoid tedious repetition. Often the best substitute for a noun is a pronoun. But beware of being over-enthusiastic and using too many variations on a particular word. The Fowler brothers, in their book *The King's English* [8], quote as many as eleven elegant variations that appeared in twenty lines of print devoted to the sale of pictures: the pictures 'made, fetched, changed hands for, went for, produced, elicited, drew, fell at, accounted for, realized, and were knocked down for, various sums'. Ingenious, but a bit over the top, don't you think?

Inversion

This is the practice of placing the verb before the subject of a sentence, or inverting its normal order of subject, predicate, object. An example is 'No sooner had he spoken than he realized he had made a grave mistake'. This inversion certainly has more effect and greater urgency than if the sentence had followed the usual construction, when it would have read: 'He realized he had made a grave mistake as soon as he had spoken'. But like elegant variation, this flourish has to be used with discrimination, or it loses its impact and leads the writer into trouble.

Idiom

Idiom is the language that is peculiar to a particular people, district, community, social group, profession, occupation, or class; it is a characteristic style of expression which may or may not follow the rules of grammar and syntax but which is acceptable as good writing if employed to add colour and create a particular impression. The scope of idiom is so wide that it is difficult to give examples, but here are a few: 'armed to the teeth', 'dead to the world', 'at the end of one's tether', 'screw up one's courage'. These are all idiomatic phrases which are expressive, bringing life to prose that might otherwise be dull and prosaic.

EXERCISES

1. What is a figure of speech?
2. What is the difference between a simile and a metaphor?
3. Name a famous allegory in English literature.
4. Give a simple definition of irony.
5. What is onomatopoeia?

Scientific prose and the scientific paper

In a book on medical writing published some twenty years ago, the author Stephen Lock, a former and distinguished Editor of the *British Medical Journal*, began one chapter with the controversial statement: 'Scientific writers are rarely literate'[9]. His argument was that too many scientists thought that only 'non-scientific second-rate minds with nothing to say' would concern themselves with style, choice of words, length of sentences, and so forth, as these were matters irrelevant to the serious scientific worker. He said that his argument could be supported by the fact that so many published accounts of important scientific work were so badly written. Coming from the former Editor of one of the leading medical journals in the world, this statement carries great weight. Let us hope that things have improved over the past twenty years, but at the same time let us take heed of his remarks.

Lock goes on to say what I have already said: that simplicity and clarity are the features of good scientific writing. It is by research that all branches of science advance, and the purpose of scientific writing is mainly to communicate to colleagues the results of research projects that may have significance for the scientific community. In medical science, of which the health sciences are an important part, there is also a need to keep professional colleagues informed about new methods of treatment, newly designed equipment, rare or unusual case histories, and advances in clinical work of all kinds; reviews of the current literature on particular topics are another useful service. For all these the writer employs the impersonal, factual style appropriate to scientific prose, although case histories benefit from a more relaxed narrative style to bring them to life and make them human.

THE ORIGINS OF SCIENTIFIC PROSE

As you already know, the first scientific journals appeared in 1665, one in France and the other, published by The Royal Society, in England. That great innovation, the printing press, had been invented in Germany in the mid-15th century by Johann Gutenberg, who printed his famous 42-line Bible in 1455. The craft of printing was brought to England by William Caxton, who had worked in a printing-house in Cologne and who set up the first printing press in this country at Westminster in 1476. He printed at least 100 books, some of them his own translations from the French, the first being *The Dictes or Sayengis of the Philosophres* (1477).

The 17th century was an era of great progress in both science and literature, and in 1660 a group of learned men meeting regularly at Gresham College, in the City of London, decided to set up a Society for Promoting Physico-Mathematical Experimental Learning. King Charles II became interested, and in 1662 granted the new Society a Royal Charter. Among the first members were such illustrious people as the scientists Robert Boyle and Isaac Newton, the architect Christopher Wren, and the poet John Dryden. Three years later, in 1665, the Society (now known as The Royal Society) launched the first scientific journal, its *Philosophical Transactions*.

Science was in those days known as 'natural philosophy', so the word 'philosophical' meant scientific. The early contents of the *Philosophical Transactions* were very varied, both in subject and merit, with archaeology and descriptions of medical curiosities proving most popular. At first, the style of writing was personal and discursive, as individual authors described their recent experiments, but as interest in scientific publication grew, a formal, impersonal style was adopted as being more appropriate to scientific discourse, and to avoid any hint of unethical self-advertisement, which in medical science was forbidden.

So developed the exact, ascetic style of writing so suited to the different disciplines that make up the world of science. At first, scientific prose may seem to you arid and restrictive, but as you become more familiar with this method of expression and with its very precise terminology, I hope you will come to appreciate and then enjoy its spare elegance as much as I do.

THE SCIENTIFIC PAPER

Every piece of scientific writing needs a structure. As the author is describing a piece of work he believes is important, he will have to explain why he embarked upon it, what methods he used to conduct the research or experiment, what answers he got to the questions he posed, and what significance they had. This is how the IMRAD format for scientific papers evolved, over a hundred years ago. With a wealth of material competing for space in their journals, editors began to demand that papers submitted for publication were well constructed, tautly written, and conveyed accurate information in the minimum number of words. Those that did not were rejected, so it behoved aspiring authors to adhere to a strict pattern.

As I explained in the first chapter, the abbreviation IMRAD stands for the initial letters of Introduction, Methods, Results, and Discussion. This is the traditional structure for a scientific paper which is still in use today, although unsuccessful attempts have been made to find other, less formal, styles. It is also a structure which serves for other purposes, as it provides a logical framework for describing any piece of work with an important or unusual outcome. Into this category come the projects, the case histories, the essays, and reports of clinical work that health science students have to complete and present to their tutors and examiners. So let us take a look at each section of this structure, to see how it should be approached.

INTRODUCTION

The sentence which starts any piece of writing must be arresting, to grab the readers' attention at the outset and make them want to read on. The first sentence in the introduction to a scientific paper is no exception. The introduction is the section where you give your reasons for embarking on the piece of work you are about to describe; you must have chosen it because it held interest for you, so a good way of beginning is to quote whatever intriguing facts or conflicting circumstances engaged your attention in the first place. The present Editor of the *British Medical Journal*, Richard Smith, gives an example in the book *How to Write a Paper*, published by his journal in 1994 [10]:

> A patient came to be anaesthetised for an operation to repair his hernia and asked whether the fact that he used Ecstasy four nights a week would create difficulties. We were unable to find an answer in published medical reports and so designed a study to answer the question.

Although this introductory paragraph was presumably written by an anaesthetist, it could equally well have been written by a nurse attending the patient, so it is an excellent model for an introduction to a paper by any health science student – simple, clear, direct, concise, wasting no words yet saying all that needs to be said about why the study was undertaken.

Yet the simplicity of this introduction is deceptive. A great deal of self-disciplined work has gone into whittling it down to the bare essentials. The temptation for a tyro writer is always to say more than is necessary, in the fear of leaving something vital out, but one has to learn to be ruthless in deciding what information is indispensable and what can be discarded as redundant. The author of the above paragraph had obviously spent many hours in the hospital library trying to find the answer to the patient's question about Ecstasy, yet he resisted what must have been a strong temptation to review the literature on interactions between anaesthetic and addictive drugs in general, as evidently none of it was directly pertinent to this case. Nor did he indulge in a historical survey of the use of Ecstasy or a description of what respiratory problems it could provoke. He gave no details of the patient's age, occupation, social group, and appearance, as these were irrelevant. In all, he was admirably succinct.

To be able to write such a good, clear, simple introduction to your paper or project, you have first to organize your thoughts carefully, and then map out exactly what you have to say in each section. During your research, you will have made copious notes. Now is the time to put them in order so that you can make a detailed plan for what you are about to write, section by section, including all the appropriate information under each heading, and discarding what is not essential. When you have completed your plan and checked it over, you can write your introduction with confidence, knowing you have done as much preparatory work as possible.

METHODS

This section may be called 'Materials and methods', or 'Patients and methods', according to the design of the study described. The word 'materials' is used to describe laboratory work or animal experiments; the word 'patients' is obviously used when the study was carried out with human beings undergoing investigation or treatment. It is here that you explain how you designed your project: how many patients were included in the study, on what basis they were selected, how they were divided into groups, over what period of time the particular investigation or treatment was under critical observation, what methods were used to elicit the data required (e.g. questionnaires, interviews), and how the data were recorded and analysed. It is also useful to mention what ethical problems you have encountered and how you solved them, and how you eliminated any form of bias from your study.

As each piece of research has a different aim, so the methodology will differ; consequently this has to be only a rough guide to what information you need to include in this section. In simple terms, having explained why you undertook the project, you now have to give a detailed account of how you set out to test your hypothesis or elicit the information you consider will make an important contribution to the 'body of knowledge'. As your tutors will tell you, it is very important that research method should be accurate, comprehensive, and reliable, so that the results obtained are valid and stand up to critical review. This methods section should also be so clear and comprehensive that someone else can carry out the same study and reproduce the same results after reading it.

In his useful book, *How to Write and Publish a Scientific Paper*, the author Robert Day emphasizes the need for precision [11]. He compares methods to cookbook recipes in which measurements must be precisely given for quantities and temperatures, for example, or culinary disaster may result. So think of your methods section as a recipe for your favourite dish, in which you must give precise measurements of all the ingredients, and precise instructions for their preparation, mixing, degree of heat and length of cooking. As you are conveying purely factual information, your style of writing will of course be appropriately terse.

RESULTS

This is the most important section of a scientific paper because it presents the findings and answers the questions that were asked at the outset. In the previous section, you have said how the data were analysed; here you give the results of that analysis and make logical deductions from them. The results of your research will probably be what you expected, but some of your findings may give you a surprise, and even prove your hypothesis wrong. This is why research is such a stimulating activity: you have to keep an open mind, and be prepared for the unexpected. This is how you learn.

In this section, you will assemble and present all the related data you have collected – the statistics; such factual information is often best presented in tables, diagrams, and figures. The presentation of statistical data in tabular form is a craft in itself, and will be dealt with separately in the next chapter. Be careful to check all your statistics for accuracy, and to check the facts given in a table against your text: you don't want an assessor to read in your paper that six men and four women took part in your study, while the table gives four men and six women!

The results section will probably be quite short, as most of the information will be compressed in the tables, diagrams, and figures. It should also be the most enjoyable to write, as you are presenting the evidence which in all likelihood proves your case. Once again, simplicity, clarity, and accuracy should be your abiding aim.

DISCUSSION

This is likely to be the most difficult section to write. Here you discuss the results of your research and compare them with findings from other research work in the same field. From this comparison, you go on to assess the value and significance of your work to your particular professional community, and suggest what further research you consider is necessary. You must also discuss your method in detail, and say honestly if it fell short in any way or produced misleading results. Your difficulty will be twofold: maintaining a balanced and objective view of your own work; and keeping the section reasonably short.

Day [11] refers to the 'squid technique': used when an author is unsure of his facts or reasoning, and 'retreats behind a protective cloud of ink' – a graphic description of smoke-screen verbiage, to be eschewed at all costs. If you find yourself rambling on in the discussion, in an effort to convince yourself of the validity of your results, stop at once, look again at your data with a coldly critical eye, and only when you are absolutely certain of their significance, and of the soundness of the logic behind the conclusions you draw, start again. It is fatal to try to hide behind a verbal smoke-screen: the only person you will deceive is yourself.

Day also tells a delightful story about a professor of biology to illustrate the dangers of scientific self-deception. This professor trained a flea to jump when he commanded it, but before writing his experiment up, he decided to take it further by removing the legs of the flea, one at a time. When the flea had no more legs, poor thing, it could not respond to his command to jump, so the conclusion the professor reached from his experiment was: 'When the legs of a flea are removed, the flea can no longer hear'!

Here, in summary, is what you have to do when writing the discussion section of your scientific paper.

1. State what your main findings are.
2. Describe any problems that arose with your methods.
3. Compare your findings with results from other work.
4. Discuss the implications of your findings.
5. Suggest what further research you consider is necessary.

COMPLETING THE PAPER

Having finished writing the main body of your paper, you will have to top and tail it, so to speak, with a title, an abstract or summary, acknowledgements to any person or organization who has helped you, and a list of references.

Title

A wordy and turgid title will not catch the reader's eye, however worthy it may be, so try to give your paper an original title that will spark off interest. It is common practice now to start with a pithy main title of two or three words only, and follow it with a longer, explanatory sub-title. Here is an example from the *Journal of the Royal College of Physicians*: 'Doctors in crisis: creating a strategy for mental health in health care work'[7]. The dramatic statement, 'Doctors in crisis', grabs the attention straight away, and the sub-title explains where the crisis is occurring without giving too much away, so that the reader wants to read on.

Abstract or summary

Many journals like to print an abstract, or précis of the contents, at the beginning of a paper. Others prefer to print a summary of it at the end. The purpose of this is to give readers a brief idea of the ground the paper covers so that they may decide how relevant it is to their own specialized field and how immediate to their interests. Practitioners in all branches of medicine are very busy people, so it helps them to know what material will be useful to them, so that they don't waste valuable time on what is irrelevant to their work.

You will have learned how to write a précis at school: it is a matter of distilling the essence from a long piece of prose, and condensing it into a few sentences – not an easy task. An abstract or summary of a scientific paper should briefly state why the work was undertaken, what methods were used, what were the results, and what was their significance. It should be interesting and informative, and no more than 250 words in length, and it should be able to stand on its own, leading the reader into the main paper, or summarizing its content.

Acknowledgements

It is a matter of courtesy to acknowledge the help you have received from individuals and organizations that was beyond the call of duty. You may have received financial sponsorship, so the funding organization should be acknowledged; a willing secretary may have typed your paper in his or her own time, and he or she too should be acknowledged; as well as senior staff who may have supervised your work or read it and made useful comments. Acknowledgements should not be written in a personal style, but in formal terms: e.g. 'The author wishes to thank Bloggs & Co. for their generous sponsorship of this research; Professor James Smith for directing the analysis of the data; and Miss Jenny Brown for help in preparation of the paper'.

References

The source of any work that is referred to or quoted in your text must be given at the end of the paper in the section that is headed 'References', and an indication must be included in the text where to find the reference made. Your tutors will tell you what system of referencing your college or university prefers; there are two principal systems, the Vancouver and the Harvard, that operate in different ways.

The Vancouver system

This is probably the most widely used system today; it uses numbers to identify published work in the text and also in the list of references. Thus if you were referring to work published by two authors, Green and Gray, you would write in the text: 'As Green and Gray reported [1] . . .', and the first item in your list of references would give the full details of their work. Thus the listed references are numbered consecutively as they appear in the text. There are standard forms of presentation for the details, one for articles and one for books. For an article, the form is as follows:

1. Green, M. and Gray, G. Rehabilitation of the lower-limb amputee: the role of physiotherapy. *British Journal of Orthopaedics*, 1996; **39**: 152–4.

As a matter of style, the titles of journals are given in italics, and may be abbreviated, as in the *Index Medicus*. The year of publication follows, and then the number of the volume of the journal (in bold type), and the page numbers on which the article appears. The volume number changes each year, and the pages in each volume are numbered consecutively.

For a book, the form differs slightly, as follows:

1. Green, M. and Gray, J. *Rehabilitation of the Lower-limb Amputee*, London, Young & Co., 1996.

The title of the book is given in italics, and is followed by the publisher's location, name, and the year of publication. The title of a specific chapter may be given after the authors' names, the title of the book is preceded by the word 'in', and the page numbers on which it appears added at the end: i.e. 'The role of physiotherapy', in *Rehabilitation of the Lower-limb Amputee* (ed. H. Ross), London, Young & Co., 1996, pp. 281–6.

The Harvard system

According to this system, references are not identified in the text by numbers but by the author's surname and the date of publication, or simply by the date: e.g. 'According to a recent report (Green, 1996) . . .'; 'As Green (1996) has reported . . .' The references are listed in alphabetical order of the authors' names at the end of the paper; the details are presented in the same way as in the Vancouver system.

While you are still a student, seek your tutors' advice about the preferred method of presenting references at your particular college or university. When you have graduated, and begin to submit work for publication, you should find out from the journals or book publishers you approach which system of referencing they use, and ask for a copy of their 'Instructions for authors', which will tell you exactly how they like manuscripts to be presented to them.

ORIGINALITY AND PLAGIARISM

It is essential to reference a scientific paper meticulously in order to avoid the sin of plagiarism – of passing off someone else's ideas or work as your own. To have credibility, published scientific work must be original, so any reference to another scientist's work must be publicly acknowledged. Not to do so can give rise to both legal and ethical problems. Legally, a breach of copyright may be committed. (The laws of copyright are dealt with in more detail in Chapter 12.) Ethically, the author has been fraudulent in stealing the fruits of someone else's labour and presenting them as his or her own.

Originality is vitally important in scientific research: new discoveries in medical science may lead to new and better methods of treatment, which in their turn will be tested and improved on, always for the benefit of patients. Integrity may be an old-fashioned concept, but in all branches of science – professional and academic – ruthless honesty is essential, both to give value and credibility to one's work and to gain the respect of colleagues.

POLISHING YOUR PAPER

When you have finished your first draft of your project or paper, you must start revising it, being slavishly self-critical and making sure you have made your meaning clear throughout. You must also be sure that all your statements are valid and your facts and figures accurate. We all have different ways of writing and revising: I use a word processor, which makes the job much easier than if you write with a pen or a typewriter, as it is so much quicker and easier to edit your own manuscript on the screen before you print it out than it is to make numerous alterations to a hand-written or type-written page.

But whatever method you use, revision is an important process. If you have the time, it is a good idea not to revise your first draft straight away, but to put it aside when you have finished it and come back to it in a day or two, when you will be able to read it more objectively and see more clearly where it needs correcting, tightening up, or even rewriting. Aim always for simplicity, clarity, and brevity: brevity is a great virtue in factual writing, not only in constructing sentences but also paragraphs. There is nothing more off-putting to the reader than having to plough through a long piece of text that is expressed in long sentences and is not broken up into paragraphs.

It is not always easy to know when to start a new paragraph. Like a sentence, a paragraph should express a complete thought, and when you have reached the end of one thought, and are moving on to another, you should begin a new paragraph. Of course, too many very short paragraphs are just as irritating as one inordinately long one, so you have to try to keep the reader's interest engaged by not labouring one point too heavily, or dealing with another too superficially. It is when you start revising your work after putting it aside for a period that you will see more clearly where you can divide a very long paragraph into several shorter paragraphs, and also perhaps introduce main headings and sub-headings to break your text up into sections and make it even easier to follow.

It may also be difficult to know when to stop revising and polishing your work. I can only say there should come a time when you know instinctively you have done all you can to make it as good as you can, and that is the moment to have the confidence to finish with it, submit it to your tutor, supervisor, or examiner, and move on to your next project.

EXERCISES

1. What do the initials IMRAD stand for?
2. What is the 'squid technique'?
3. What five points should be made in the discussion?
4. What points should an abstract contain?
5. How should references be indicated in the text?

Using illustrations

There is a saying in journalism that one picture is worth a thousand words, and even in a serious scientific paper or article an illustration can often convey information more succinctly and more vividly than words. If you are writing a case history, for example, a photograph showing the patient's disability before and after treatment, or comparing the normal with the abnormal in a certain condition, can say more in less space than a lengthy verbal description.

There are a number of ways in which a piece of scientific prose can be illustrated: by tables, graphs, charts, diagrams, and photographs. As we saw in the last chapter, this applies to presenting statistical data in the 'Results' section of a research paper in the IMRAD format, but it also applies to any piece of writing a health science student is required to do: an essay, project, case history, research report, or dissertation. All will benefit from carefully prepared illustrations which enhance the text by presenting information concisely in visual form.

GENERAL RULES

There are certain general rules which are worth following if you are to use illustrations to the best effect.

1. Every illustration must say something: it must contain and convey information that is relevant to the topic.
2. No illustration should simply repeat what is in the text.
3. All illustrations should add to and clarify the text.
4. All illustrations should be well presented, simple, and easy to understand.
5. Every illustration should be able to stand on its own, explained by its caption or legend.
6. All illustrations should be introduced, or at least referred to, in the text, and placed as close as possible to that reference.

In short, be selective in your use of illustrations, making sure they add something to the text instead of merely repeating it. Don't put too much information into tables or charts; keep them simple so that they are clear and easy to understand. Accompany each illustration with a brief 'legend' which explains what it shows. When writing legends, or captions, for photographs, don't just say what is obvious to the reader's eye (e.g. 'Fig. 1: A woman with spinal fractures') but give some additional information about the subject of the photograph (e.g. 'Fig. 1: A 72-year-old woman with three fractured vertebrae due to osteoporosis of the spine').

Tables are numbered consecutively and referred to in the text as such (e.g. 'see Table 1'). All other illustrations, whether they be photographs, charts, diagrams, or graphs, are referred to as Figures, and also numbered consecutively. The abbreviation 'Fig.' is usually used in the legend, though in the text the complete word is mostly used (e.g. 'see Figure 1').

Now let us look at each type of illustration separately, and discuss how to present it effectively.

TABLES

A table is an excellent way of presenting statistical data and other factual information in a concise form which is easy to take in at a glance. Say that you have been doing a project on that humiliating affliction, incontinence, and want to enumerate the different causes of urinary incontinence in women. Instead of itemizing them all in one long sentence, you can present them in a table, introducing it thus: 'The common causes of incontinence in women are listed in Table 9.1', placing the table (below) as close to this reference as possible.

Table 9.1 Common causes of urinary incontinence in women

- Genuine stress incontinence (urethral sphincter incompetence)
- Detrusor instability
- Detrusor hyperreflexia
- Overflow incontinence secondary to urinary retention
- Fistulae (vesico-vaginal, uretero-vaginal, urethro-vaginal)
- Congenital lesions (e.g. epispadias, ectopic ureter, spina bifida)
- Urethral diverticula
- Temporary causes (e.g. urinary tract infection, faecal impaction, confusional states)

Reproduced with permission from the Royal College of Physicians, *Incontinence: causes, management, and provision of services*; published by the Royal College of Physicians of London, 1995 [12].

You could then go on to discuss the causes in detail under each heading listed.

This is a simple table presenting factual information. A more complicated one will be required for presenting numerical data, for example how many children in a group studied were found to have faecal incontinence. In constructing this table, you have to remember that people read from left to right, and from top to bottom, so the subjects studied should be listed vertically, and the statistical information should flow under different headings from left to right. Here is an example.

Table 9.2 Percentage of children with faecal incontinence

| Percentage still lacking bowel control by the birthday in question: | | | | | |
2nd	3rd	4th	5th	6th	7th
boys					
56.9	11.0	4.3	3.5	2.9	2.4
girls					
43.2	5.2	1.4	1.0	0.8	0.7
both					
50.2	8.1	2.8	2.2	1.9	1.5

Reproduced with permission from the Royal College of Physicians, *Incontinence: causes, management, and provision of services*; published by the Royal College of Physicians of London, 1995 [12].

Now you can discuss the statistics shown, and the possible reasons why more boys than girls in the study were found to be unable to control their bowels over time.

Tables should be introduced by a concise legend stating what they are intended to show. All information included should be kept as brief as possible, but if unfamiliar abbreviations are used they should be explained in a footnote. Measurements used should also be explained in a footnote if necessary. Each table should make only one point, and the reader should be able to grasp all the information given at first sight. Don't use too many rules in your tables. Horizontal rules above and below the table, and beneath the heading or legend, are usually all that are needed; it is not necessary to use vertical rules to divide columns from each other.

GRAPHS

Graphs are used to present numerical data which show trends or comparative relationships, usually over a period of time. More than one line or curve representing a trend can be shown on a graph, up to a maximum of four; more than four would be very confusing to follow, particularly if the lines crossed at any point. It is more accurate to join points on a graph by straight lines rather than curves; although curves look better, they can be misleading.

The abscissa (horizontal axis) and the ordinate (vertical axis) should always be calibrated. The independent variables should be plotted on the horizontal x axis, and the dependent variable on the vertical y axis. It is the convention always to show measurements of time on the horizontal axis.

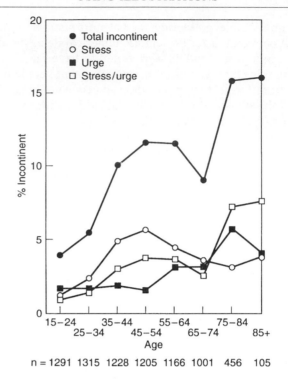

Fig. 9.1 Example of graph, showing the prevalence of stress, urge, and stress/urge incontinence in women by age. Redrawn from Mandelstam, *Incontinence and its Management* (2nd edn); published by Croom Helm, 1986 [13].

Lines on a graph should be differentiated from each other, either by colour or by using solid, dotted, or broken lines, and these should be identified in the legend or on the graph. The symbols normally used to show different points on a graph are circles, triangles, and squares, either solid or in outline. These, too, should be identified. The same symbol must, of course, be used within each line plotted.

Each graph should be accompanied by a brief and explicit legend explaining its purpose, and any wording on the graph should be kept to the minimum. Continuing with our imaginary project on incontinence, as an example here is a graph (Figure 9.1) showing the prevalence of incontinence from four different causes among women by age. Different symbols have been used to identify the lines for the different causes of incontinence.

CHARTS

There are several types of chart, the most frequently used being bar charts (sometimes called bar graphs), histograms, pie charts, and flow charts.

Bar charts are a useful alternative to tables and graphs for presenting numerical data in visual form. The bars show data for one variable, and can be either vertical or horizontal. As a time scale will be given on the horizontal axis, a horizontal bar would be used to show when an event occurred during that particular period of time. A vertical bar chart could be used in place of a complicated graph to show comparative trends or relationships more clearly, the bars being identified by different colours or by hatching, dots, or shading.

Histograms are similar to bar charts, but show continuous data rather than individual observations. Examples of a bar chart and of a histogram are given in Figures 9.2 and 9.3. As with all illustrations, each should be

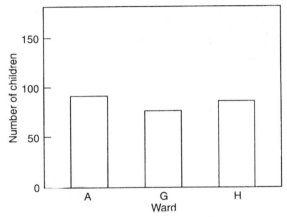

Fig. 9.2 Example of a bar chart, showing admission rates of children to a ward during June 1992. Redrawn from Taylor, *Study Skills for Nurses*; published by Chapman & Hall, 1992 [14].

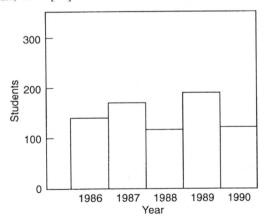

Fig. 9.3 Example of a histogram, showing number of student passes in physics over 5 years. Redrawn from Taylor, *Study Skills for Nurses*; published by Chapman & Hall, 1992 [14].

accompanied by a brief and explicit legend stating its purpose, and accurate measurements.

Pie charts are so called because they are circular and divided into sections, like slices of a pie, to show how proportions of a whole compare in size. The 360° circle representing 100% can be sliced into percentage portions, as you can see in the example shown (Figure 9.4), and each portion labelled and differentiated by hatching, dots, or shading. A key to the method of differentiation must be included, as here.

Flow charts are a type of algorithm, or diagram showing a step-by-step procedure for solving a problem or reaching an objective where there are

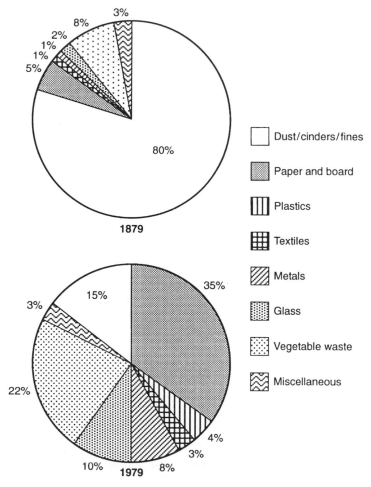

Fig. 9.4 Example of a pie chart, showing the increase in the disposal of waste. Redrawn from Caddow (ed.), *Applied Microbiology*; published by Scutari Press, 1989 [15].

alternative paths. A flow chart starts by stating the main problem and then follows a path punctuated by decisions leading to different courses of action. Returning to the topic of incontinence – a major problem for the elderly – Figure 9.5 is a flow chart showing how urinary incontinence in elderly people should be managed.

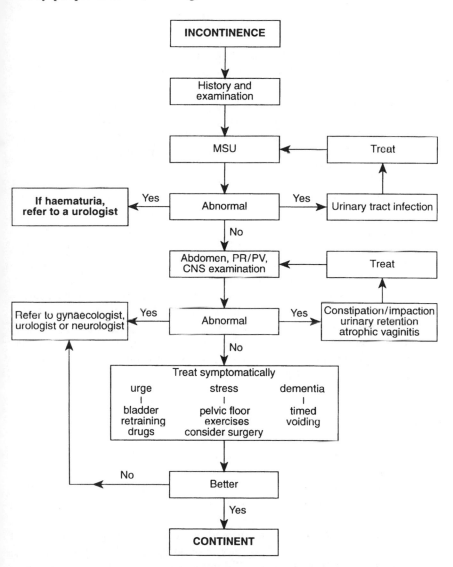

Fig. 9.5 Example of a flow chart, showing the management of urinary incontinence in elderly people. Redrawn with permission from the Royal College of Physicians, *Incontinence: causes, management, and provision of services*; published by the Royal College of Physicians of London, 1995 [12].

Flow charts may also be presented in list form, in the form of family trees, or as circuit diagrams. Again, as with all illustrations, they should be clear and easy to follow, adding to and not repeating the text, and accompanied by a concise and lucid legend.

PHOTOGRAPHS

A good photograph can say more than any number of words describing a patient with a deformity or disability, or an unusual type of skin disease, for example. Photographs are obviously particularly effective in illustrating case histories: showing the patient from the initial examination through the various stages of treatment to recovery of whatever degree of normality is possible. Don't forget, though, that each photograph must say something explicit, and add visual impact to the text. Never include a photograph just because it looks nice!

You must always ask patients for their permission to be photographed, and explain your purpose in doing so as a matter of courtesy. They also appreciate being offered copies of any photographs taken. It is common practice to mask the eyes of patients in photographs being published, in order to conceal their identity. A close-up shot will show detail better than a long-distance shot, and it is important to get good focus and clear definition, if you are taking your own photographs. Colour photographs are obviously valuable in showing details of a condition – such as a rash – in which colour is significant, but black-and-white prints often give clearer definition than colour. X-ray plates can be printed up in black and white.

Writing good captions, or legends, for your photographs is not an easy task. Resist the temptation merely to say what the photograph shows: try and add some useful and pertinent facts.

DIAGRAMS

A really well-drawn anatomical diagram is hard to beat as an illustration for a clinical paper, because it shows clearly and precisely all that a photograph cannot show, and illustrates the text helpfully. For example, Figure 9.6 shows exactly how in men an enlarged prostate gland can obstruct the flow of urine.

Diagrams of pieces of equipment, and devices such as joint replacement prostheses, can show more detail than photographs, and are easier to label to indicate the component parts. All diagrams should be carefully drawn to proportion, and clearly labelled. If you are not gifted at precision drawing, it is better to trace an existing diagram from a textbook which has been drawn by a professional artist. Don't forget to acknowledge the source of

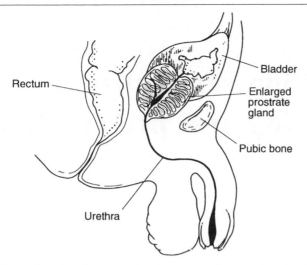

Fig. 9.6 Example of a diagram, showing prostatic hypertrophy. Redrawn with permission from Norton, *Nursing for Continence*; published by Beaconsfield Publishers, 1986 [16].

the drawing, however, as the copyright remains with the artist and the publisher. If diagrams are reproduced in published work from published work, permission has to be obtained first from the publisher, and a proper acknowledgement made of the original source (as, for example, in Figure 9.6). A fee may also be payable.

IN CONCLUSION

Like scientific prose, scientific illustrations of all types should be clear, simple, and informative. They should add to and amplify the text, and aid the reader's understanding.

EXERCISES

1. Give the six general rules for using illustrations.
2. Describe the different types of illustration, and state the purpose of each.
3. How should you go about writing a caption or legend for a photograph?
4. How should the different types of illustration be referred to in the text?
5. What is meant by abscissa and ordinate?

| 10 | # Writing exam answers and making oral presentations |

There are two ordeals students have to face during their training which are nerve-racking in a similar way. One is the unseen written examination, the other is making an oral presentation before an expert audience, and both demand the particular skill of accumulating knowledge on a specific subject and storing it in the memory so that one can write or speak lucidly, accurately, and succinctly on a chosen topic without reference to textbooks or notes, and usually within a specified period of time – not easy!

WRITTEN EXAMINATIONS

Everyone dreads the prospect of sitting a written exam. No matter how thoroughly you have done your revision, you are always certain the examiners will have set questions that will find all the gaps in your knowledge, and you will be sure that, as soon as you sit down at the desk in the examination hall, your mind will go blank and all the carefully stored facts will vanish from your memory bank. Don't despair! There are ways of preparing for and coping with the ordeal which should help to overcome the natural temptation to panic.

Preparing for an exam

As this is a book about writing, it is not the place to discuss such things as how to do your revision, or the need to get a good night's sleep before an exam. It is the place to start thinking about your approach to writing exam answers, which will be different from your approach to other pieces of written work you have to produce. You have to start thinking about your readers – the examiners – and what they are looking for in your answers to their questions. They are testing the depth and breadth of your knowledge, and their assessment will be influenced by your ability to aim at a very expert readership and express yourself clearly and comprehensively, and to support your arguments with authoritative evidence.

On a very practical note, as examination answers are written in long-hand, make sure your handwriting is legible. So many students use word processors or typewriters nowadays that it is easy to let handwriting become untidy and ill-formed through lack of use. A little practice in handwriting in the days and weeks before an exam will help you to improve it and make it neat and easy to read. Your answers may be absolutely brilliant, but it's not going to help you to get good marks if the examiners can't read them!

It is a good idea to get hold of previous exam papers in the subjects you will be taking, so that you can study the type of questions asked and the level at which they are pitched. Try answering some of them as part of your revision: this will give you the opportunity to practise writing at the length required. Writing an exam answer is very different from writing an essay or a research report. For one thing, it will be considerably shorter, probably not more than 500 words. You can work out the length from the time allowed for the examination, the number of questions you have to answer, and the time it takes you to write. Some people write quickly, others slowly, so it will help you to time yourself while you are writing a practice answer, so that you know how long it will take you to produce 500 legible words.

Writing concisely, which you have to do in an exam, is quite an art in itself. You have to learn to cut out any non-essentials, anything which could be classed as 'waffle', any tendency to wordiness or woolly thinking, anything which is not germane to your argument, and to be ruthless in jettisoning what you may regard as your best pearls of prose. You have to concentrate on presenting the relevant facts clearly and precisely, as you know them, and on quoting reliable sources of reference to support your case.

Writing to length is something that journalists have to do all the time, and it is a very disciplined form of writing, often maligned in academic circles. There are limits, of course: I remember, when I was working on the editorial staff of *Radio Times*, being told to write about a broadcast of Handel's *Messiah* in 150 words. When I angrily rebelled against this restriction, the Editor put me in my place by telling me: 'Words are just something to keep the pictures apart'! But it was a very good training in using only words that have a particular meaning and convey a specific message to the reader.

Journalists also have to meet deadlines, and this too is what you have to do in examinations – write against the clock. It should help you to read and analyse feature articles in the quality newspapers and magazines on topics that interest you. A great deal is currently being written about controversial issues in the National Health Service, such as whether expensive treatments should be rationed and offered only to those patients who will have a long-term benefit from them. Feature articles in national newspapers are rarely longer than 500 words, so it would be well worth your while to study one you find particularly interesting, to analyse both the content and the writing, and see what you can learn from it. Then try to write an article of a similar length on a similar topic, giving yourself a reasonable time limit, and compare it with the piece written by a professional journalist.

You will probably find that the journalist has said more in fewer words than you have. That is the art of writing concisely: choosing words that say what you mean simply and clearly, without any additional padding. There are a lot of words that you can dispense with because they are auxiliaries, not principal performers. To show you what I mean, here is a paragraph I once wrote on osteoporosis which could do with some editing.

> Medical experts contend that during their teens, when youngsters should be consuming at least 1,200mg of calcium per day, many unfortunately get barely half that amount. One reason is the obsession that teenage girls have with dieting, which can lead to the eating disorders anorexia and bulimia nervosa, which are increasingly common among adolescent girls. Overdieting can often result in loss of menstrual periods as well as rapid loss of bone density, leading to fractures and osteoporosis.

Here is my own edited version.

> Doctors believe that many teenagers get barely half the amount of calcium they need per day – 1,200mg – because they are obsessed with dieting. Overdieting can cause anorexia and bulimia nervosa, loss of menstrual periods, and rapid loss of bone content, leading to fractures and osteoporosis.

I have cut 33 words out of the original 77, and I am sure you will agree it's an improvement, and demonstrates how to simplify and get rid of redundant words without losing any of the sense.

Try to give yourself some practice at writing against the clock. It's largely a matter of keeping your nerve and making the best use of the time available. Don't waste time panicking but spend it usefully on planning what you want to say, making notes if that helps you, and then getting down to writing with as much confidence as you can muster.

In the examination hall

The most important thing, once you are seated at a desk in the examination hall and the invigilator has given you the go-ahead, is to read the examination paper carefully, at least twice, before deciding which questions to answer. This will give you time to consider exactly what the questions mean and what information or argument they seek to elicit. Examination questions are carefully phrased, and if you don't give time to understanding them you may go off on the wrong track and lose marks. Time spent in concentrated thought at this stage will benefit you in the end.

When you have chosen your questions, analyse each one carefully, identifying the subject and which aspect of it you should cover, note the instructions you must follow – i.e. 'discuss', 'evaluate', 'compare and contrast' – and look for any significant words in the question which may give you a key to its meaning, and point you in the right direction.

Written exam questions are sometimes called 'essay' questions, as opposed to 'multiple choice' questions (MCQs) which don't require long written answers. So prepare a plan for each question, as you would for an essay, using the scrap paper which will doubtless be supplied. It's a good idea to make notes for an essay plan for each question before you start to answer the first one, as some of them may overlap. Also some universities take essay plans in note form into account if you don't manage to finish a paper in the time allowed, as evidence of the ground your written answer would have covered.

Many exam questions in the health sciences involve factual knowledge, but some may require you to make judgments between, say, two courses of action or methods of treatment. In answering such a 'judgment' question, you must first define the problem, identify the two sides of the argument, then present a case for each side, with supporting evidence, and finally make your own judgment, explaining your reasons for reaching that conclusion. In both types of question – factual and judgmental – you must exhibit a knowledge of the literature, so that the examiners will know you have studied the relevant texts. Some universities and colleges allow students to take reference books into examinations, but others do not, so it is sensible to memorize the authors and titles of the main works of reference you may need to quote in your answers.

You should also be prepared to illustrate your answers with tables, charts, and diagrams, as appropriate, so some preparatory work in doing free-hand illustrations will pay off. The neater you can make them look, the more impressed will the examiners be.

As with all scientific writing, examination answers should be expressed in simple, clear, and direct language, but above all they must be concise and to the point, yet as comprehensive as you can make them. The secret of achieving this is to begin by defining your limits, and then to keep within them. Each answer should be well constructed, with a beginning, a middle, and an end. It should be neat, easy to read, and well presented, as well as clearly expressed. It should do justice to your abilities, and show evidence of your knowledge.

MAKING ORAL PRESENTATIONS

Speaking in public, if only to a small seminar group, is another ordeal students have to face. As a health science student you will have to present case studies of particular patients, or make a poster presentation, or act as a spokesperson for a group of fellow students in a seminar. Whatever the occasion, you will have to get up on your feet and speak articulately to your audience on a specific topic without either boring or embarrassing them.

Public speaking is another difficult art that doesn't come easily and has to be learned if it is to be effective. There is both physical and mental preparation to be done: the mental preparation includes deciding what you want to say, structuring your thoughts into a logical sequence of argument, and memorizing the background to the points you want to make; the physical preparation covers learning how to breathe and project your voice, how to articulate your words clearly, how to stand, and how to gesture.

Mental preparation

The public speaker who simply reads a prepared text, head down and eyes on the script, is not going to make much of an impact on the audience, so the first thing you have to do is be prepared to speak only from notes or headings. This is not to say you need not write out your speech beforehand – it depends what method you find helps you most – but when it comes to the moment of truth, when you are on your feet ready to speak, you must be able to make eye contact with your audience and speak to them directly and spontaneously.

Don't be deceived by speakers who make it look easy and natural. They can only do this because they have done a lot of hard homework beforehand, so that they know their subject almost backwards, and can speak on any aspect of it fluently and convincingly. This is what you have to learn to do.

When you have been given, or have chosen, the topic for your talk, mull it over in your mind for a while to give yourself an opportunity to decide what you want to say. Then start writing down any points you want to include, as they come into your mind or as you come across them in your textbooks or notebooks. When your ideas have taken shape you can arrange these points in order and begin to give your talk a structure – a beginning, a middle, and an end.

When you have made as many notes as you need, you can begin to write your talk out in full, if you think this will help you. Personally, I prefer to move on to the next stage of making headings and listing the points I want to make under each heading. The danger of writing out the text of a talk is that you will simply memorize it and its spontaneity will be lost, or you will take it with you when you have to speak and end up by reading it. In making oral presentations, the ability to speak on your subject 'off the cuff' without referring to notes will demonstate your grasp of it far better than reading from a script, however well written it is. This approach is certainly nerve-racking, and it needs a good deal of practice to get it right, but the results are undoubtedly much better.

But whether you prefer to write out your talk or not at this stage, the next one is to make a heading for each paragraph or section, and list the points you want to include under each heading. This is best done on a series of postcards, with one postcard to each heading, and carefully numbered in the right order. If you get them out of order, you could be in trouble! Now try giving your talk to a few long-suffering friends using these postcards, and you may be surprised at how fluent you can be – provided you really know your subject well. You should be able to keep eye contact with your audience, only glancing down at your cards now and then to remind yourself what is the next point you are going to discuss. Practise until you feel you can do this quite confidently.

Physical preparation

There is much more to speaking in public than just getting up and talking to whomever may be in the same room. First of all, you want to be sure that everyone can hear what you have to say, and this means learning how to control your breathing so that you can support your voice and project it out of your mouth to the very back of the room or hall. It also means learning how to form your words properly by using your lips, tongue, and teeth, and the muscles round your mouth, to pronounce the consonants and vowels that make up words. It is particularly important to sound the consonants at the ends of words so that they can be heard: it is irritating to listen to a slovenly speaker who swallows the final consonants or uses the glottal stop too freely instead of sounding the 't's. As a student you will have to speak to tutors and examiners who won't be impressed by such poor delivery. When you are qualified you may have to talk to patients, to your professional colleagues, or to groups of students on a teaching round, with the purpose of giving them important factual information or demonstrating a certain method of treatment, so you must be able to make yourself clearly understood. There is no room for lazy or self-indulgent speech here, and learning how to speak well in public during your training will be a great advantage to you when you are launched on your career.

For the same reason, it is important now to get into the habit of using the spoken word properly, avoiding the overworked jargon words and phrases such as 'well', 'like', 'you know', and 'I mean' that interrupt the flow of verbal expression far too frequently. Instead, try to form your spoken sentences as carefully and accurately as your written ones.

Breathing

If you are speaking for any length of time, and having to make your voice audible throughout a large room or hall, the first thing you need is plenty of breath. Deep breathing, and filling the base of the lungs with air so that there is always a reserve to fall back on, is the first necessity. Shallow or costal breathing is useless for voice production. Actors and singers who have to produce and control their vocal tone have first to learn breath control. As you all know, after air has been inhaled into the lungs, it is exhaled by a contraction of the diaphragm muscle which forces breath up through the larynx and pharynx and out through the mouth or nose. For an extra supply of air to support the voice, you need to expand the lower part of the rib cage and draw as much air as you can into the base of your lungs, while the diaphragm relaxes. Then you need to expel the air from your lungs by slow and controlled contraction of the diaphragm.

Here is an exercise for deep breathing. Place your hands flat on each side of your chest, at the base of your rib cage, with the tips of the middle fingers just touching. Breathe in slowly and deeply and the fingertips will part as air descends into your lungs. Breathe out slowly by consciously contracting the diaphragm, and your fingertips will touch again. The further apart you can force the fingertips of your two hands, the more air you are breathing into your lungs. Now breathe in to a count of three, hold your breath for a count of three, and breathe out to a count of three, making sure you have got rid of all the breath in your lungs. Next do this exercise while walking at a steady pace – in to a count of three steps, hold for three steps, out for three steps, and hold for three steps. If you do this regularly, you will soon learn how to control your breathing, and to make sure you can speak a long sentence without taking a breath in the middle.

Articulating

Again as you all know, vocal tone is produced by air being forced up through the vocal cords, which lie at the top of the larynx, through the resonators (the pharynx, the mouth, and the nose) and out through the mouth. Vowels and consonants are formed by movements of the facial muscles, lips, the tongue and the teeth. These are known as the organs of speech. If you are to speak clearly, these movements must be performed properly – not lazily, but in a slightly exaggerated way so that every part of every word is articulated and the words themselves can be clearly heard.

If you study voice production, as I have, your teacher will give you all sorts of strange exercises to do that will make your organs of speech more mobile and elastic. One that loosens your lips and the muscles round your mouth is to blow like a horse so that the lips vibrate against each other. Try it! Another that makes the lips, tongue, and soft palate really work is to repeat the weird refrain, 'Ningy, nongy, noo', as many times as you can without feeling a complete fool. Any student who is studying speech therapy will know many more that can assist articulation. The object is to make the movements of the lips and tongue against the teeth more precise so that vowels and consonants are given their full value.

Different groups of consonants are formed by different mouth movements. There are the 'explosive' consonants, P and B, T and D, K and G, which are made by the lips alone, by the tip of the tongue against the upper teeth, and by the back of the tongue against the soft palate respectively. There are the 'fricatives', F and V, TH, and SH, made by the upper teeth and lower lip, the tongue tip and teeth, and the tongue tip and both upper and lower teeth. Then there are the nasal consonants, M and N, which use the lips alone, and NG, which is formed by the back of the tongue and the soft palate – not forgetting the sibilants, which are hissed by the tip of the tongue against the teeth. If you practise producing all these different types of consonant, you will find your speech organs are working really hard. There are many different exercises in alliteration that you probably learned as a child, such as the old favourite 'Peter Piper picked a peck of pickled pepper', which help to produce good consonants. Try making up a few tongue-twisters, like 'mixed biscuits', which will really make you work hard if you repeat them quickly several times over.

For good articulation and projection, you need to place the voice forward in your mouth, and open your mouth wide to enable it to fly out as far as it can. Don't keep the sound at the back of your mouth, because you will simply swallow it and what you are trying to say will be inaudible. Never forget that a speaker who produces the voice really well should be able to whisper and still be heard at the back of the room.

Posture and relaxation

Physiotherapy students will know all about good posture, and the need to stand up straight before starting to speak in order to be able to breathe well. They will also know the importance of being relaxed, getting rid of all nervous tension, before embarking on this ordeal.

Nervous tension can affect the voice, so relaxation techniques should be part of your physical preparation. When you do get up to speak, you want to look relaxed and at ease, so stand with your feet slightly apart, and with your weight balanced between them. Try not to shift your weight continually from one foot to the other, which is distracting to the audience, but stay as still as you can, moving only to handle your postcards, or to point to some visual display you are using. If you need to make any sort of gesture, make a definite one and don't be afraid to make a big one. Arm and hand gestures should always be made above the waist, where they can be easily seen. Hand-waggling gestures at hip level are merely irritating, and add nothing to any sort of talk.

Finally, the best piece of advice to all tyro speakers is the classic imperative: 'Get up, speak up, and shut up'. In other words, know what you want to say, say it clearly and with confidence, don't waffle, be reasonably brief, and come to a definite conclusion. Then you stand a good chance of getting and keeping your audience's attention until you have finished.

EXERCISES

1. What is the secret of writing concisely?
2. What is the first and most important thing to do in an exam?
3. What is a 'judgment' question, and how should it be answered?
4. Should the text of a talk be written out in full?
5. What is the classic advice to speakers?

Writing essays, case studies, and research reports

The written work required of health science students varies according to which professional training course they are taking, and which college or university they are attending, as each has its own curriculum and methods of assessment. There are certain pieces of work, however, that are common in essence if not in detail, such as essays, case studies and patient profiles, and reports of research studies or projects, laboratory experiments, and health education leaflets of one kind and another. This chapter will offer some general advice on how to tackle the different written projects that are common to most training courses in the health sciences.

ESSAYS

An essay is a literary genre in which the writer expresses his or her personal opinions in short but elegant prose on a chosen topic. Literary essays can be witty and entertaining, or profound and philosophic: who has not chuckled over Charles Lamb's 'Dissertation upon Roast Pig', or struggled with Sir Francis Bacon's 'Of Truth'. An academic essay, of the kind students have to write, demands a different style and technique. While it is written on a specific topic, and often contains expression of an individual's opinion, its purpose is to demonstrate the writer's knowledge and understanding of the subject to the tutor or examiner. Essays may be short or long, from the 500-word examination answer we have already discussed, to the 8000-word extended essay that is often part of the Finals assessment, but whatever the length, writing an academic essay requires a particular approach.

You know, from reading the previous chapter, how important it is in a written examination to read the questions carefully. This is equally important when writing a course-work essay, as the question or topic you are given will be carefully worded to elicit a particular type of answer. There are two main kinds of essay: the **factual** essay, in which you have to provide factual information on the relevant aspects of the subject; and the **judgment** essay, in which you have to identify any conflicting aspects of the topic, present the arguments for each one, balance them against each other, and use your objective judgment to make a choice between them. Sometimes, as in an **integrated** essay, you may have to combine the two approaches, drawing first on your factual knowledge of, say, the systems of the body, and then weighing up and selecting from the different approaches to treatment of a particular condition affecting one particular system. You must, of course, support your argument with textual evidence.

Analysing the question

The first thing you have to do is decide what the subject of the question – and therefore of your essay – is, and what sort of essay you are expected to write. This will be determined by the way the question is phrased and what instructions it gives you. For example, if a factual essay is required, you will be asked to outline, or describe, or compare and contrast particular aspects of the subject. If a judgment essay is wanted, the question will ask you to discuss or evaluate a certain statement or set of circumstances related to the subject. Here are examples of the two types of question.

Factual: 'What are the common causes of incontinence in women?'

This essay question tests your knowledge of the female genito-urinary system and the main factors that can adversely affect its functioning. The key word is 'incontinence', and the subject of your essay is what causes women to be incontinent. Note the word 'common' in the question: this means you must restrict yourself to describing the principal causes, and omit those that are rare.

Judgment: 'Recent data suggest that a moderate intake of alcohol protects against coronary heart disease, so the "sensible" limits of alcohol intake should be relaxed. Discuss.'

This essay question raises a number of points to test your knowledge and understanding of the topic, and your judgment. You need to know what the 'sensible limits' for alcohol consumption are (14 units a week for women, 21 units a week for men); why these have been applied and by whom; who has recently suggested they should be relaxed and to what levels; who is resisting this move and why. Finally, you need to weigh up both sides of the argument and draw your own conclusions.

The temptation you must resist when embarking on an essay is simply to write as much as you know about the subject. This is not what will get you good marks. Examiners certainly want to know that you have a good bedrock of knowledge, but they also want to find out how well you understand the subject, and whether you can analyse it and discuss its different aspects. They want to know if you have good objective judgment, and can see the implications of a decision, perhaps between two methods of treatment, as they may affect the patient and the family. So read the essay question carefully, look for key words in it, be clear in your mind what instructions it gives you, and then follow them to the letter, not allowing yourself to digress.

The essay plan

When you have done your research and gathered your material together, the next step is to plan your essay point by point. This means making a list of main headings, in a logical sequence, which you can use to break up your text into sections. Under each main heading you should list the points you wish to make as sub-headings. Your first paragraph will act as an introduction, and your last as a conclusion, and in between you will develop your argument, paragraph by paragraph, each self-contained but leading on to the next. Thus before you start to write, you will have created a definite structure for your essay to give you both limits and flexibility.

You may use your introductory paragraph to repeat that part of the question that poses a problem or introduces an issue that needs to be defined. In defining the problem, you will mention the aspects of it that have implications you propose to discuss. This will lead you into your next paragraph and the first main point for discussion. That paragraph should link with the next and the second point you make, and so on, so that each paragraph, while self-contained and expressing a single thought, leads on to the next, until all your main points are made. Your final paragraph will draw the main threads of your argument together, and give you the opportunity to sum up and present your own conclusions. You should quote references throughout your essay to support your statements and arguments.

Presentation

An important aspect of essay-writing is presentation. An essay that is neat, clean, legibly written, and accurately spelt will make a much better impression than one that is untidy and difficult to read. It goes without saying that good grammar and syntax are essential.

All colleges and universities have their preferred methods of presentation, as your tutors will tell you, but in general it is usual to use A4 paper, lined if your essay is hand-written, when you would write on every second line to leave space for your tutor's comments. If you use a typewriter or word processor, your essay should be double-spaced. You should also leave wide margins on each side of the page, again for your tutor's remarks. Write on one side of the paper only, and start with a title page giving your tutor's name in one corner, then the title of your essay and your own name in the centre of the page. It is also helpful to add the title of your course, and the date you finished the essay and handed it in. Don't forget to number your pages consecutively, so that they can be put back in order easily if they should get separated. You could even develop the journalist's habit of writing your surname before the number on each page, as below:

Young – 13.

If the pages of several essays get separated and mixed up, this identification makes sorting them out much easier.

If you are including tables and diagrams, they should be neatly drawn, well captioned, numbered consecutively, and referred to in the text by their respective numbers – 'Table 3', 'Figure 1', etc. Tables are referred to as tables, but other illustrations, whether charts, graphs, diagrams, or photographs, are referred to as figures. You should insert them in the text as close to the reference as possible. If they are too large to fit into the page, indicate clearly in the margin where they should go, and attach them to the page.

Your text must be properly referenced, using either the Harvard or the Vancouver system, or whatever system your university or college prefers. The published work quoted should be referred to in the text by a number or by the author's surname and date of publication, and a complete list of the references should be given at the end of your essay, either in numerical or alphabetical order, according to the system used. A bibliography may also be given with extended essays: this is a list of all the published work you have read and that is relevant to the subject of the essay. It is essential to get the details of the published work absolutely right, so that anyone could trace the books or articles in a library. We have already looked at how references should be presented in Chapter 8, and we will go into this in greater detail in Chapter 12.

Style

Essays should be written in a formal, impersonal style, avoiding use of the personal pronoun. For example, instead of writing, 'I hope that . . .', you would write, 'It is to be hoped that . . .'. If you find yourself using the passive voice too frequently, you can use the active voice with that impersonal pronoun 'one': 'one hopes that . . .' or 'one has seen . . .'. If you are not careful, using 'one' can sound a little pompous, so be aware of that risk.

Headings which identify the subject-matter that follows are always helpful to the reader, and break the text up into sections. Headings come in different 'weights', and are usually displayed in different ways: for instance, a main or 'A' heading can be presented in CAPITAL LETTERS above a paragraph; a 'B' heading can be in ordinary 'lower case' letters underlined above the paragraph; and a 'C' heading can be underlined and start the paragraph, with the text running on after it. If you are using a word processor, you can experiment with bold (very heavy) type and italics to distinguish the relative weight of your headings. But once you have decided on a style for them, be consistent and stick to it, so that the reader becomes familiar with it.

Make sure your sentences are well constructed, and that your words are well and accurately chosen, meaning exactly what you want to say. Your paragraphs should be neither too long nor too short, but each contain a single thought which is linked to the one before and the one that comes after. Discard any redundant ideas, no matter how appealing, so that your essay is taut and economic. Stick to the point of your argument, keep your sense of direction, and don't wander off into the thickets of irrelevancy. Keep your sentences short and expressive, and if you find yourself rambling on, remember that the full stop is the writer's best friend.

When you have finished your first draft, read it over carefully, checking your facts and your spelling for accuracy. If time permits, put it away for a day or two and come back to it with a fresh mind, when you are bound to see points of style and content that you need to change or correct. One minor point: if you use a word processor with a spell-check facility, try not to rely on it too heavily, or you will get out of the habit of checking your own spelling, which will be a disadvantage in written exams.

CASE STUDIES

Patients are people, not cases, but what is written about them individually is still termed a 'case study' or a 'case report' or a 'case history'. The more human term 'patient profile' is emerging, but whatever you like to call it, the study of an individual patient which reveals all the problems concerning his or her illness or injury lies at the core of all medical, nursing, and paramedical practice.

All health science students will have to write a case study at some time in their training, to show how they can apply theory to practice. As sick and disabled people are the focus of all patient care, and are endlessly fascinating in the wealth of problems they provide for the professionals to solve, writing a case study can be both absorbing and rewarding.

In compiling a case study, you should present the relevant information in chronological order. You start by giving brief details of the patient – name, sex, age, occupation, domicile, etc. – and follow these with the presenting symptoms. Next come details of the examinations and investigations carried out, the results of these, and the diagnosis made. Last will come the treatment recommended. If physiotherapy, occupational therapy, speech therapy, podiatry, or any other remedial therapy is prescribed, a student studying any of these disciplines will be expected to make an assessment of the patient's needs and abilities, to state the aims of treatment, to recommend the methods of treatment that are most appropriate to the individual case, and to outline the expected outcome. A student nurse will be expected to devise a nursing care plan, and to monitor and report on the patient's progress.

Writing a case study will, of course, test the student's knowledge of the condition the patient is suffering from, and of the organs or body system affected. More importantly, perhaps, it will test the student's ability to perceive the patient as a whole person, with psychosocial problems which may have an effect on the recovery process, or may even have been a factor in causing the illness. There is a strong link between psychological stress and a number of physical conditions, for instance, and often nurses and therapists are best placed to perceive the existence and nature of such problems through their continued contact with the patient. The ability to see beyond the end of your own nose is vitally important to a practitioner of any of the health professions and this is what you as health science students must demonstrate in writing a case study.

As a case study is descriptive, telling the story of a patient, a narrative style of writing is most suitable. While the personal details of the patient will be fully described, the writer's style should remain as impersonal and objective as possible, avoiding any sentimental or emotive language. This may be difficult, as it is natural to respond sympathetically to human problems, but a careful balance has to be struck between human understanding and emotional involvement.

RESEARCH AND PROJECT REPORTS

The longest and most important piece of writing you will have to do as an undergraduate is the report of a project or research study carried out in your final year which will be assessed for your Finals results. The length of this report will vary according to the requirements of your college or university, but it will equate to an extended essay and could be anything up to 10 000 words long. You will be able to choose the subject for this research project yourself, with the guidance of your tutor or supervisor, who will also help you to give it a good title, and provide advice and support when you ask for it.

You read in Chapter 8 how the IMRAD format for writing scientific papers developed, and this format will provide the basis for the report of your research project, with some additions. The purpose of this report is to test your knowledge of the subject you have chosen, your ability to present information and ideas through the medium of the written word, and to complete a long and comprehensive piece of work in a given time. It will also give you a chance to show your initiative and originality of thought, as well as your objective judgment and capacity for sustained accuracy.

Your place of learning will undoubtedly supply you with guidelines for presenting this research report, but the usual format is to start with a title page, giving your name and perhaps an identification number, the name of your college or university, the name of the course the work relates to, the full title of the work, and the date you have submitted it. After this will come – not necessarily in this order – a list of contents giving the headings of the different sections and their page numbers; a list of acknowledge-ments; and an abstract. Then will follow the report itself in its formal sections: introduction, literature survey, methods, results, discussion, and conclusions. The report will end with the list of references, bibliography, and appendices (if any). Here is an at-a-glance list of contents:

Title page
Acknowledgements
List of contents
Abstract
Introduction
Literature review
Methods
Results
Discussion
Conclusions
References
Bibliography
Appendices

I must repeat that this list is only a guide, as each university or college will have its own requirements and the number and order of these sections may differ.

Title

It is important to have a good, arresting title for your project; your tutor or supervisor will help you here if you have any difficulty.

Acknowledgements

Here you should acknowledge the help of anyone who has gone beyond the call of duty, so to speak, or to whom you particularly want to express appreciation. But don't make this section sound like an embarrassing acceptance speech at a film or television awards ceremony!

Abstract

This is a brief précis of the content of your report, saying why you chose the subject, what you set out to achieve, how you collected your data, what results they showed, and what conclusions you drew from them. It should aim to capture the interest of readers, and make them want to read on.

Introduction

This will set the scene for your research project, giving your reasons in full for deciding to carry it out, and describing its purpose and scope. It may include the literature review, if the idea for it sprang from a study of the literature on the subject: you may have seen a gap which needed to be filled by a further study, for example.

Literature review

If this is not included in the introduction, it should show that you have read not only widely but also discriminatingly on the subject of your study. In other words, it should include only texts that have relevance to your topic, and that you can show have contributed to your thinking on it.

Methods

You must explain clearly the methodology you have chosen, and demonstrate that it is valid, appropriate, and will produce accurate data. You should mention any ethical problems involved, and describe how these have been solved. If you decided to do a pilot study in advance of the main study, you should state this here and describe any changes that have been made as a result, and the reasons for them.

Results

These must be presented clearly and objectively, without any bias. Statistical data can be presented more clearly and briefly in tables, charts, and diagrams than in written text, but beware of putting too much into a table or chart; keep them simple and easy to assimilate at a glance. If you are drawing any illustrations yourself, make sure they are neat and readable. Don't forget that all tables and figures should be numbered consecutively, captioned, and referred to in the text by their numbers. Don't repeat what you have written in the text in your illustrations, but make each one self-contained, adding something to the text. Place each illustration as near as possible to the reference to it in the text. Acknowledge the source of 'borrowed' illustrations.

Discussion

This is the section in which you interpret the results obtained from the data collected, and discuss their implications. They may or may not prove the validity of the theory you expounded in your introduction, and here you must be ruthlessly honest, allowing absolutely no personal bias to creep into your discussion. Here you must also discuss any faults that were revealed in your methodology, and how they could be remedied. If the results you obtained did not support your hypothesis, you must analyse and explain the reasons for this. Writing this section is a test of your objective thinking, and you must not allow yourself to be disappointed if your theory is not proved: that very fact may provide useful knowledge leading to further valuable research.

Conclusions

In this final paragraph, you should summarize the main points of your report and of your discussion, evaluate your main findings, and suggest any further research you believe is indicated.

References and bibliography

These must include full details of the work quoted, presented in the required style, and adhering to that style completely and accurately.

Appendices

These will consist of extra relevant background material, and should be numbered in order: Appendix 1, Appendix 2, and so on.

Style

The writing style for such a research report should be disciplined and formal, in the third person, and entirely suitable for a scientific paper. Learning to write in this way now will benefit you greatly after you have qualified. A word of warning about plagiarism: this is to quote the work of another writer as if it were your own, without making proper acknowledgement of its original source. Doing so in a published paper could be a breach of copyright, for which you could be sued. Doing so in an academic paper for assessment for your degree could have an equally disastrous result. So if you are quoting from another's work, be sure to say: 'As Bloggins wrote . . .', and include the reference; or if you are using an illustration from some published work, acknowledge the source; otherwise you could be in big trouble.

OTHER COURSE WORK

There may be other written course work you have to produce, such as health education leaflets for patients, but the three major projects I have described should provide a good basis for all your other written work. A word about writing for lay people (patients) may be useful: try to avoid using any medical or technical terms they may not understand, or if you do use them, explain them in lay language in the same breath. Use simple, short words and sentences, and be direct in your method of expression. Imagine that a lay person you know well personally is one of your patients, and write for him or her. Then you will probably produce something lucid and helpful.

EXERCISES

1. What are the two types of essay, and how do they differ?
2. Why is making an essay plan important?
3. How should an essay be presented?
4. How should headings be displayed?
5. What styles of writing are suitable for (a) an essay, (b) a case study, and (c) a research report?

Writing dissertations and theses | 12

During your undergraduate years you may have become interested in the research process, and want to follow it up. To develop a hypothesis and test it by rigorous scientific investigation is, as the late great medical scientist Sir Peter Medawar put it, an 'adventure of the mind', and one that you can pursue as a postgraduate student. The first step on this path is to take a Master's degree, which may involve both course work and research and which will require the student to write a dissertation, usually about 20 000 words long. The second step is a doctorate: a full research degree for which you have to write a thesis of about 80 000 words in length. To be eligible for acceptance to read for either of these degrees the intending postgraduate student has to meet the academic standards laid down by individual colleges or universities.

What is the difference between a thesis and a dissertation, apart from length? My dictionary defines a dissertation as 'a long, detailed, usually written treatment of a subject'; and a thesis as 'a dissertation embodying the results of original research'. It is the requirement for originality that distinguishes the thesis from the dissertation, since someone submitting a thesis for examination for a doctorate is expected to offer research findings that contribute something new and valuable to the body of knowledge in a specific field of study.

Bearing that in mind, when it comes to the actual writing of a dissertation or thesis the approach is very similar, though a thesis will of course demand a greater degree of sustained thinking, concentration, and interest over a longer period of time because of its length. For a thesis, therefore, it is vital to choose a topic which will not only hold but also increase its interest for you, and offer the opportunity for original ideas and innovative findings. It is perfectly possible to choose a topic for a Master's degree dissertation which affords scope for development into a Doctoral thesis: I have done this myself, and it is helpful to find, when embarking on the research for a doctorate, that one has done a good deal of the spadework already, and discovered the potentialities for further excavation.

A thesis or dissertation in one of the health sciences will follow the well-tried IMRAD format, and be similar in structure to the report of a research project (discussed in the previous chapter). It will be longer and more detailed, as the research it describes will have been more extensive. To write at this length – the length of a book – requires sustained mental effort over a long period: the capacity for dogged hard work rather than flashes of intellectual brilliance. You also have to remember that now you are writing not only for the closed world of tutors and examiners, but also for members of your profession, and possibly of related professions, who may find your work interesting or useful – or may wish to challenge your findings. Your language and method of expression must consequently be unfailingly simple, direct, and explicit, and your accuracy unassailable.

PRELIMINARY PLANNING

Like a book, a thesis or dissertation requires careful planning. Having chosen your topic and decided how to approach it, you have to give your ideas shape and structure, and divide your material into different sections, or chapters. Here the IMRAD format gives you a basic structure which you can adapt to meet your own needs as well as the requirements of your academic institution. You will first be required to give your thesis a provisional title, and to prepare a research outline. In your introduction you should explain why you have chosen this topic, how you propose to set about your research, what facilities you will need, what resources you will use, what work has recently been done in the same field that might overlap with yours, and how you can add to it. You should then give a detailed account of the research method you propose to adopt, and outline the possible findings and their implications for professional practice.

Your supervisor will give you help and advice in producing this research outline, which has to meet the academic standards for postgraduate research of your college or university.

STARTING TO WRITE

Once your research outline has been approved, you can start work in earnest – and this means writing as well as doing your research. Instead of waiting until you have collected and analysed all your data, and your research is completed, it is better to start writing as soon as you can, while the material is fresh in your mind. It doesn't matter at this stage if it is not properly organized or arranged; it is better to get your thoughts down early, section by section, in a first draft which you can revise and reorganize when all the work is finished. Then you will be able to bring a critical eye to bear on it, and correct and reshape it where necessary.

Producing some written work regularly for your supervisor to see and comment on helps both of you. It gives your supervisor an idea of your progress, and the opportunity to offer guidance and suggestions; and it gives you a regular opportunity to talk about your work with your supervisor, seek advice, discuss problems, and make progress in the right direction. A good relationship with your supervisor will give you the feeling of security you need in what can be a lonely academic existence.

Writing is always hard work, even for professional authors, so another advantage of writing regularly is that you will get into the habit of it, and be able to break the back of your mammoth task – for that is what a doctoral thesis is – much more quickly than if you had left the writing until all the practical work was completed. Then it would loom ahead like a vast and forbidding mountain that was impossible to climb.

It may help you to keep a day-to-day diary while you are doing your research, so that when you come to write up a section of your thesis you have a complete record of all your experiments and observations to draw on. This, too, will help to make writing easier, and the words to flow more fluently.

THE STRUCTURE

Each university has its own requirements for the presentation of theses and dissertations, and will send details of these to all postgraduate students some months before the work is due to be submitted for examination. These instructions will cover such practical details as the number of copies required, and how the manuscript should be typed and bound, but they will also describe how the thesis should be arranged. A typical example (from my own university, Sussex University) is:

Title page
Declaration (to meet university regulations)
Preface (to meet university regulations)
Summary
Titles of Chapters and Appendices (if any)
List of Abbreviations
List of Illustrations, Figures, Maps, and Tables
Chapters
Bibliography
Appendices (if any)

The student will also be sent the university's regulations for the award of research degrees, which may contain rules governing the content and presentation of the thesis (as above).

The main content of a thesis will then consist of the introduction, setting out its aims; a survey of the literature; a description of the materials and methods used; the results obtained; the analysis and discussion of those results; and the conclusions drawn by the author from them. This follows closely the IMRAD format (explained in Chapter 8), so needs no further explanation here. What does deserve some repetition is advice regarding use of other people's work, and the presentation of references and bibliography.

PLAGIARISM

Plagiarism is the sin of passing off someone else's work as your own, which is an offence against university regulations. If undetected, the sin would amount to acquiring a degree under false pretences. It could also amount to a breach of copyright: work published during an author's lifetime is protected for 70 years after the author's death, and it is an infringement of copyright to quote part of a protected work without permission from the author and/or publisher. Any quotation from a published work must be properly acknowledged.

The same rule applies to the reproduction of illustrations from published work. Should you wish to use a figure or table from a current textbook, you must give the details of the title of the book, the name of its author and publisher, and the page on which the illustration appears. You should also write to the publisher of the book to request permission to use it; the publisher will get the author's permission, and may give you a form of words to use as an acknowledgement of their permission and the source of the work. Publishers sometimes also charge a fee if illustrations are reproduced in commercial work.

REFERENCES AND BIBLIOGRAPHY

It is for this reason, as well as to enable readers to follow up the sources you quote, that it is vitally important to make sure your manuscript is properly referenced: that is to say that, under whatever system your university or college requires you to use, you acknowledge any work quoted by including in the text either the author's name and the date of publication of the book and article, e.g. (Young, 1996), or the number of the work as it is listed at the end of your manuscript, e.g. [13].

As you already know, there are two principal systems of referencing, the Harvard and the Vancouver. The Harvard system uses the author's surname and the date of publication in the text or, if the author's name has already been mentioned, only the date of publication. The references are listed at the end of the chapter (or sometimes of the whole manuscript) in alphabetical order of authors' names. The Vancouver system uses numerals to identify references in the text, e.g. [13], and lists the references in consecutive numerical order.

It is worth repeating here how the details of referenced work should be presented, as it is extremely important to get this right – not only in your academic work, but also later when you may be submitting work for possible publication. As you will see from the textbooks and journal articles you quote, all have their own preferred style of presentation, to which authors must slavishly adhere, and most use either the Vancouver or the Harvard system.

Apart from their different methods of identification and listing, and subject to 'house style', both systems use the same method of presenting the details of the published work, though there are slight differences between books and journal articles, as follows.

Books

The author's surname is given first, then initials, then the title of the book, then the edition (if this is not the first), then the publisher's location, the publisher's name, and lastly the year of publication. Here is an example:

> Young, P.H. *The Art and Science of Writing* (3rd edn), London, Chapman & Hall, 1996.

If there is more than one author, list them all in the order given on the title page. If you are referring to a chapter in a book edited by another author, you would present it thus:

> Josephs, C. Drug therapy and the elderly, in *Nursing the Aged* (ed. P.H. Young), Cambridge, Woodhead Faulkner Ltd, 1984, pp. 48–58.

It is common practice to underline titles of books, and they are usually set in italics when printed. It is also common practice to give the first and last pages of a chapter in a book, as I have here.

Journal articles

The author's surname is given first, then initials, then the title of the article, followed by the title of the journal (underlined or in italics), the year of publication, the volume number (in bold or heavy type), and the page numbers. If there is more than one author, list them all, though some journals limit the number of authors' names to three, the others being covered by the anonymous '*et al.*'. Here is an example:

Young, P.H. Smoking and the young. *The British Journal of Nursing*, 1992; **1**: 648–651.

The title of a journal article or of a book chapter may sometimes be given in quotation marks, according to the style preferred by the institution or publisher.

You may wish to cite unpublished work in your references. If it is a book or article that has been accepted for publication but is not yet published you would put after the title 'In press'; if the work has been written but has not yet been accepted for publication, after the title you put 'In preparation'. If you are citing a document or letter sent directly to you, you give the author's name and initials and put 'Personal communication' in place of a title. Interviews with individuals should be listed separately, under the heading 'Interviews', giving the name of the interviewee and the date and place of the interview.

The details of published work listed under 'Bibliography' should be given in exactly the same way as for references.

FOOTNOTES

You should resist the temptation to add footnotes to a page to explain or support a point, because they merely distract the reader's attention from your main text. Anything you think you should put in a footnote should be incorporated in the text, if possible. Some authors have such an addiction to footnotes that they can take up more of the printed page than the text itself, and how irritating that is for readers!

ABBREVIATIONS

I would remind you that you should only use abbreviations, however familiar they are, after writing out what they stand for in full. Then you can place the abbreviation in brackets directly afterwards, and use it thereafter. An example is National Health Service (NHS).

STYLE

By this time, you will be well practised in writing scientific prose, so I will only reiterate my main theme: short, direct, simple words and sentences demonstrate clear, straight, and accurate thinking. It is much more difficult to write simply and clearly than to use long, tortuous sentences and a plethora of technical jargon which merely obfuscate your meaning. But it is well worth the effort, as your examiners will appreciate having a 'good read' instead of having to plough through interminable passages of turgid prose.

And don't worry if your thesis is shorter than the length specified. This is a maximum length, not to be exceeded, and examiners will welcome a piece of work that is commendably concise, elegantly written, and perfectly presented – as yours is bound to be.

EXERCISES

1. What is the difference between a dissertation and a thesis?
2. How should a dissertation or thesis be structured?
3. What are the advantages of writing as you go along, rather than waiting until your research is completed?
4. What is plagiarism?
5. What is breach of copyright?

13   Epilogue: writing for publication

The art of writing scientific prose is as essential to the qualified practitioner as it is to the health science student. Once qualified and launched on a professional career, the practitioner has a responsibility to share new knowledge and ideas with colleagues through writing for the professional journals, and the information contained in this book should equip you (and, I hope, encourage you) to set out on the path to publication.

There is nothing more satisfying than seeing your words in print, and if you have had something unusual or controversial to say, it is rewarding when your readers respond – even though their comments may be critical. At least they have bothered to read and react to what you wrote, and you may be able to start a debate that stimulates new thinking.

Professional journals now abound in the field of health care, so there is plenty of scope and opportunity for new writers, provided they have some original ideas to offer. A good way of getting your foot in the literary door is to write a letter for publication commenting on an article or other material a journal has published. If your letter is sufficiently pithy and well expressed it should stand a good chance of acceptance, and once your name has appeared in that journal a couple of times, it is worth submitting a short article for publication.

Don't be discouraged if your first literary attempts are rejected; this has happened to most writers, and your motto has to be: 'If at first you don't succeed . . .'. It's always worth asking the Editor why your article has been turned down, so that you can learn from the reasons given and change your approach accordingly. Although Editors are very busy people, the good ones will always find the time to help and encourage potential new contributors with something interesting to say.

If you are successful, and get bitten with the writing bug, it is a good idea to study the various journals in your field, to see the particular style of content, writing, and presentation each one prefers, and model your material accordingly. Most journals provide printed 'Instructions to authors', and will send them on request to intending authors. The Editor will naturally be better disposed towards an article carefully written and presented in the style of the journal, and suited to its content, than towards a submission by an author who has not bothered to present it acceptably.

If you become known as a writer on a specialized subject, your writing career can blossom. Other journals may ask you to contribute articles, review books, or report conferences for them, and if you show you have the depth of knowledge and command of language required, a publisher might ask you to write a book. If you are skilled in the art and science of writing, the professional world can be your oyster. I hope I have opened the door to that world for you.

Answers to Exercises

CHAPTER 2

1. 'The patient did not want to take any medication', or 'No medication would be accepted by the patient'.
2. If you are referring to a group of people as a single entity, use the singular; if you are referring to them as a group of individuals who may be mentioned individually subsequently, use the plural.
3. When the flow of the sentence would be adversely affected if you didn't.
4. 'Shall' when used with the first person is the future tense; when used with the second and third persons it denotes a threat or promise. Conversely, 'will' when used with the first person denotes a threat or promise, and with the second and third persons is part of the future tense.
5. An 'absolute' is a word that does not admit of degrees, so it can **never** be qualified.
6. Well, better, best; much, more, most; badly, worse, worst. There are others.

CHAPTER 3

1. A group of words which makes sense, **or** A combination of words which is complete as expressing a thought.
2. The verb 'to be'. 'It is me' is often wrongly used for 'It is I'.
3. Main clause, co-ordinate clause, subordinate clause, noun clause, adjectival clause (relative clause), adverbial clause.
4. A clause is constructed on the 'subject–predicate–object' pattern, but a phrase is not.
5. Two main clauses linked together by a conjunction.

CHAPTER 4

1. To show that items enumerated are separate and not linked.
2. (a) To join two main clauses together that are connected; (b) to separate phrases in enumerations.
3. Its special function is to deliver the goods that have been invoiced in the preceding words.
4. Spell out in full the expression for which the abbreviation is used, and give the abbreviation in brackets after it.
5. The correct use is to indicate that a letter is missing. It should not be used before a plural 's'.

CHAPTER 5

1. It resembles good manners.
2. Appropriateness, perspicuity, accuracy, persuasiveness.
3. The last, 'Prefer the Saxon word to the Romance', because Romance words derive from Latin, which is the derivation for many scientific terms.
4. Practical and practicable, militate and mitigate.
5. Confused, unintelligible, outlandish or barbarous language.

CHAPTER 6

1. A tautology repeats the meaning of the word preceding or following it. A pleonasm uses more words than are necessary to convey the sense intended.
2. A participle that is not attached to the noun or pronoun that is the subject of the verb.
3. A sentence should end with a strong word; a preposition is too small and weak to bear the responsibility.
4. Words related to each other must agree in gender, number, and case.
5. It depends on the antecedent: 'who' should be used after a person, 'which' after an inanimate object, and 'that' after a thing that has human connotations, e.g. an event or organization.

CHAPTER 7

1. A way of enhancing meaning and making it more vivid.
2. Simile makes a specific comparison between two things; metaphor implies a resemblance.

3. John Bunyan's *Pilgrim's Progress*.
4. Saying one thing and meaning another.
5. A word that simulates a sound: e.g. hiss, croak.

CHAPTER 8

1. Introduction, Methods, Results, and Discussion.
2. Smoke-screen verbiage: hiding doubt in a cloud of ink.
3. (a) What the findings are; (b) any problems with methods; (c) comparison of findings with others in the same field; (d) significance of the findings; (e) what further research is indicated.
4. Why the work was done, what methods were used, what the results were, what significance they had.
5. Under the Vancouver system by a figure in brackets; under the Harvard system by the author's name and date of publication, also in brackets, or by the date of publication only if the author is mentioned in the text.

CHAPTER 9

1. (a) Every illustration must say something. (b) No illustration should repeat the text. (c) All should add to and clarify the text. (d) All should be simple, clear, and easy to understand. (e) Each illustration should stand on its own. (f) All should be introduced or referred to in the text.
2. Tables, graphs, charts, photographs, diagrams. Tables, graphs, and charts present statistical data in different ways. Photographs and diagrams add a pictorial dimension to the text.
3. Don't simply state what the reader can see; add some useful information.
4. Tables are referred to as such; all other illustrations are referred to as Figures. Both are numbered consecutively.
5. In a graph, the abscissa is the horizontal axis and the ordinate the vertical axis. Both should always be calibrated.

CHAPTER 10

1. Choose words that say what you mean simply and clearly, without any additional padding. Avoid waffle!
2. Read the examination paper carefully at least twice before choosing the questions to answer; then analyse each chosen question equally carefully before starting to write.
3. A 'judgment' question expects you to weigh up two courses of action,

sides of an argument, or methods of treatment, to present a case for each, and to make your own judgment as to which is preferable, giving your reasons to support your choice.

4. It helps some people to write a talk out in full beforehand and then memorize it, but it is better to be able to speak from headings and sub-headings, written in note form on postcards. This helps you to get a really firm grasp of your subject and to speak directly and spontaneously on it.

5. 'Get up, speak up, and shut up!' This means standing up straight, looking your audience in the eye, speaking clearly and audibly, being reasonably brief, and coming to a definite conclusion.

CHAPTER 11

1. Factual and judgment: a factual essay is descriptive, presenting factual information, while a judgment essay is discursive, presenting conflicting points of view between which you have to make a balanced judgment.

2. It provides a structure for the essay before you start to write, providing both limits and flexibility within them.

3. On A4 paper, double-spaced, with wide margins, written on one side of the paper only, the pages numbered consecutively. Above all it should be neat, legible, and correctly spelt.

4. In different weights – A, B, and C – for main, sub-, and side headings. A different typeface or style should be used for each.

5. (a) Impersonal, (b) narrative, (c) strictly disciplined and formal.

CHAPTER 12

1. A thesis submitted for a doctorate is expected to contain original ideas and findings that will add to the body of knowledge.

2. The IMRAD format – introduction, methods, results, and discussion – forms the basis of the thesis structure, with the addition of a summary or abstract, conclusions, references, bibliography, appendices (if any), and any other sections specified by the academic institution.

3. (a) You break the back of the work more quickly; (b) you can discuss your written work with your supervisor regularly; (c) you get into the habit of writing, and become fluent sooner.

4. Passing off someone else's work as your own – an offence against academic regulations.

5. All published work is protected up to 70 years after an author's death, and it is an infringement of copyright to quote from an author's work without permission and acknowledgement.

References

1. Leacock, S. *How to Write*, London, John Lane The Bodley Head, 1944.
2. Gowers, E. *The Complete Plain Words*, London, Penguin Books, 1962.
3. Quiller-Couch, A. *On the Art of Writing*, London, Guild Books, 1916.
4. Fowler, H.W. *A Dictionary of Modern English Usage* (2nd edn), Oxford, Clarendon Press, 1965.
5. Carey, G.V. *Mind the Stop*, London, Penguin Books, 1971.
6. Waterhouse, K. *English Our English*, London, Viking (Penguin Books), 1991.
7. Higgs, R. Doctors in crisis: creating a strategy for mental health in health care work. *Journal of the Royal College of Physicians*, 1994; **28**: 538–540.
8. Fowler, H.W. and Fowler, F.G. *The King's English* (3rd edn), Oxford, Oxford University Press, 1973.
9. Lock, S. *Thorne's Better Medical Writing* (2nd edn), London, Pitman Medical, 1977.
10. Smith, R. Introductions, in *How to Write a Paper* (ed. G.M. Hall), London, BMJ Publishing Group, 1994.
11. Day, R.A. *How to Write and Publish a Scientific Paper* (3rd edn), Cambridge, Cambridge University Press, 1989.
12. The Royal College of Physicians. *Incontinence: causes, management, and provision of services*, London, RCP, 1995.
13. Mandelstam, D. (ed.) *Incontinence and its Management* (2nd edn), London, Croom Helm, 1986.
14. Taylor, J. *Study Skills for Nurses*, London, Chapman & Hall, 1992.
15. Caddow, P. (ed.) *Applied Microbiology*, London, Scutari Press, 1989.
16. Norton, C. *Nursing for Continence*, Beaconsfield, Beaconsfield Publishers, 1986.

Further reading

Carey, G.V. *Mind the Stop*, London, Penguin Books, 1971.

Day, R.A. *How to Write and Publish a Scientific Paper* (3rd edn), Cambridge, Cambridge University Press, 1989.

Fowler, H.W. and Fowler, F.G. *The King's English* (3rd edn), Oxford, Oxford University Press, 1973.

Gowers, E. *The Complete Plain Words*, London, Penguin Books, 1962.

Hall, G.M. (ed.) *How to Write a Paper*, London, BMJ Publishing Group, 1994.

O'Connor, M. *Writing Successfully in Science*, London, Chapman & Hall, 1991.

Partridge, E. *Usage and Abusage*, London, Penguin Books, 1973.

Taylor, J. *Study Skills for Nurses*, London, Chapman & Hall, 1992.

Turk, C. and Kirkman, J. *Effective Writing* (2nd edn), London, Chapman & Hall, 1989.

Waterhouse, K. *English Our English*, London, Viking (Penguin Books), 1991.

FOR REFERENCE

Fowler, H.W. *A Dictionary of Modern English Usage* (2nd edn), Oxford, Clarendon Press, 1965.

Lloyd, S.M. (ed.) *Roget's Thesaurus*, Harlow, Essex, Longman, 1982.

Oxford English Dictionary Dept. *The Oxford Dictionary for Writers and Editors*, Oxford, Clarendon Press (Oxford University Press), 1981.

Index

Page numbers appearing in **bold** refer to exercises containing questions which relate to that particular subject.